ACTIVITY WORKBOOK

SIDE by SIDE

THIRD EDITION

BOOK 3

Steven J. Molinsky
Bill Bliss

with

Carolyn Graham

WITHDRAWN

Contributing Authors

Dorothy Lynde • Elizabeth Handley

Illustrated by

Richard E. Hill

Side by Side, 3rd edition
Activity Workbook 3

Pearson Education, 10 Bank Street, White Plains, NY 10606

Vice president, director of publishing: *Allen Ascher*
Editorial manager: *Pam Fishman*
Vice president, director of design and production: *Rhea Banker*
Associate director of electronic production: *Aliza Greenblatt*
Production manager: *Ray Keating*
Director of manufacturing: *Patrice Fraccio*
Associate digital layout manager: *Paula D. Williams*
Editorial supervisor: *Janet Johnston*
Digital layout specialist: *Lisa Ghiozzi*
Interior design: *Wendy Wolf*
Cover design: *Elizabeth Carlson*

Illustrator: *Richard E. Hill*

The authors gratefully acknowledge the contribution
of Tina Carver in the development of the original
Side by Side program.

Longman on the Web
Longman.com offers classroom activities, teaching tips and online resources for teachers of all levels and students of all ages. Visit us for course-specific Companion Websites, our comprehensive online catalog of all Longman titles, and access to all local Longman websites, offices and contacts around the world.

Join a global community of teachers and students at **Longman.com**.

Longman English Success offers online courses to give learners flexible, self-paced study options. Developed for distance learning or to complement classroom instruction, courses cover General English, Business English, and Exam Preparation.

For more information visit **EnglishSuccess.com**.

ISBN 0-13-026875-5

Printed in the United States of America

17 18 19 – CRK – 11 10 09

CONTENTS

A WHAT'S HAPPENING?

| what | bake | cook | move | sit |
| where | compose | go | read | watch |

1. A. _____What's_____ Fran ___reading___ ?

   B. _____She's reading_____ her e-mail.

2. A. _____Where's_____ Fred _____?

   B. _____ to the clinic.

3. A. _What's_ Nancy _Watching_ ?

   B. _She's watching_ a game show.

4. A. _What are_ you _cooking_ ?

   B. _I'm cooking_ dinner.

5. A. _Where are_ you and your wife

   moving ?

   B. _We're moving_ to Miami.

6. A. _where are_ your grandmother

   and grandfather _sitting_ ?

   B. _They are sitting_ in the park.

7. A. _what is_ Victor _composing_ ?

   B. _He's composing_ a symphony.

8. A. _What are_ you _Baking_ ?

   B. _I'm Baking_ an apple pie.

1.

A. Hi. What _____are_____ you doing?

B. _____I'm watching_____ a movie on TV.

A. Oh. I don't want to disturb you. _____Is_____ Anna busy?

B. Yes, _____she is_____. _____She's taking_____ a bath.

A. I'll call back later.

2.

A. Hi, Bill. _____are_____ the children okay?

B. Yes. _____They're_____ fine.

A. What _____are they_____ doing?

B. Vicky _____is doing_____ her homework, and

Timmy _____is playing_____ baseball in the yard.

A. How about you? _____What are_____ doing?

B. _____I'm cooking_____ dinner for you and the kids.

A. I'll be home soon.

3.

A. Hello, Peter. This is Mr. Taylor. _____Is_____ your father at home?

B. No, _____he isn't_____. _____He's_____ at the health club.

A. Can I speak to your mother?

B. I'm sorry. _____She's_____ busy right now. _____She's fixing_____ the washing machine. It's broken.

A. Okay. I'll call back later.

4.

A. Hello, _____. Can I speak to _____?

B. I'm sorry. _____.

A. Well, can I speak to _____?

B. I'm afraid _____.

A. Okay. I'll call back later.

1. *(clean)* I never _____clean_____ my apartment, but _____I'm cleaning_____ it today

   because _my grandmother is going to visit me (or) my boss is coming over for dinner_.

2. *(iron)* Roger never _____ his shirts, but _____ them today

   because _____.

3. *(argue)* We never _____ with our landlord, but _____ with him today

   because _____.

4. *(worry)* I never _____ about anything, but _____ today because

   _____.

5. *(watch)* Betty never _____ the news, but _____ it today because

   _____.

6. *(write)* Uncle Phil never _____ to us, but _____ to us today

   because _____.

7. *(take)* I never _____ the bus, but _____ it today because

   _____.

8. *(comb)* My son never _____ his hair, but _____ it today

   because _____.

9. *(get up)* My daughter never _____ early, but _____ early today

   because _____.

10. *(smile)* Mr. Grimes never _____, but _____ today because

    _____.

11. *(bark)* Our dogs never _____, but _____ today

    because _____.

12. *(wear)* Alice never _____ perfume, but _____ it today

    because _____.

1. I recommend the fish.

   Do you recommend the chicken, too?

2. My husband bakes delicious cakes.

   _____ he _____ pies, too?

3. My daughter gets up early.

   _____ your son _____ early, too?

4. They always complain about the traffic.

   _____ they _____ about the weather, too?

5. Maria speaks Italian and Spanish.

   _____ she _____ French, too?

6. My grandson lives in Miami.

   _____ your granddaughter _____ there, too?

7. I watch the news every morning.

   _____ every evening, too?

8. My sister plays soccer.

   _____ tennis, too?

9. Robert practices the trombone at night.

   _____ during the day, too?

10. We plant vegetables every year.

    _____ flowers, too?

11. Stanley always adds salt to the stew.

    _____ pepper, too?

12. I always wear a jacket to work.

    _____ a tie, too?

13. My cousin Sue rides a motorcycle.

    _____ a bicycle, too?

14. My grandfather jogs every day.

    _____ when it rains?

15. We need bread from the supermarket.

    _____ milk, too?

16. Gregory always irons his shirts.

    _____ his pants, too?

17.

Our neighbors have three dogs.

_____ any cats?

Across

3. I like to cook. I'm an excellent _____.
4. I can type. I'm a very good _____.
5. Sally swims fast. She's a fast _____.
6. Jeff likes to play sports. He's a good _____.
7. My sons drive taxis. They're both taxi _____.

Down

1. You ski well. You're a very good _____.
2. We act in plays and movies. We're _____.
5. My children love to skate They're wonderful _____.

F WHAT'S THE ANSWER?

Circle the correct answer.

1. Does Hector like to play tennis?
   a. Yes, he likes.
   b. Yes, he does.
   c. Yes, he is.

2. Are you a graceful dancer?
   a. No, I don't.
   b. No, you aren't.
   c. No, I'm not.

3. Does your boss work hard?
   a. Yes, he is.
   b. Yes, he does.
   c. Yes, he works.

4. Is the food at this restaurant spicy?
   a. Yes, it isn't.
   b. Yes, it does.
   c. Yes, it is.

5. Are your children good athletes?
   a. Yes, I am.
   b. Yes, they are.
   c. Yes, they do.

6. Do you and your girlfriend like to cook?
   a. Yes, she does.
   b. Yes, they do.
   c. Yes, we do.

7. Am I a good teacher?
   a. Yes, you are.
   b. Yes, he is.
   c. Yes, you do.

8. Does your husband send e-mail messages to you?
   a. Yes, he is.
   b. Yes, he does.
   c. Yes, she does.

1. A. I _____don't_____ like to eat at Albert's house because he _____ cook very well.

    B. I know. Everybody says he _____ a very good _____.

2. A. I know you _____ like to drive with me because you think _____ a terrible driver.

    B. That's not true. I think you _____ very carefully!

3. A. _____ like to type?

    B. No, I _____. _____ not a very accurate typist.

    A. I disagree. _____ an accurate typist, but you _____ very slowly.

4. A. Oliver Jones is an excellent composer.

    B. I agree. He _____ beautifully. I think _____ very talented.

5. A. Irene _____ going swimming with us today because she _____ like to swim when it's cold.

    B. That's too bad. I really like to go swimming with her. She's a very good _____.

6. A. I'm jealous of my classmates. They speak English very well, and I _____.

    B. That's not true. Your classmates _____ English clearly, but you're a good

    English _____, too.

H **LISTENING**

Listen to each question and then complete the answer.

1. Yes, _____he does_____ .

2. No, _____she isn't_____ .

3. Yes, _____ .

4. Yes, _____ .

5. No, _____ .

6. Yes, _____ .

7. No, _____ .

8. Yes, _____ .

9. No, _____ .

10. Yes, _____ .

11. No, _____ .

12. Yes, _____ .

13. Yes, _____ .

14. No, _____ .

15. No, _____ .

1 GRAMMARRAP: *Does He Like the Movies?*

Listen. Then clap and practice.

A. Does he like   the movies?

B.   No,   he doesn't.   He likes   TV.

A. Does she like   the mountains?

B.   No,   she doesn't.   She likes   the sea.

A. Do you like to   hike?

B.   No,   I don't.   I like to   dive.

A. Do they like to   walk?

B.   No,   they don't.   They like to   drive.

A. Is he studying   music?

B.   No,   he isn't.   He's studying   math.

A. Is she taking   a shower?

B.   No,   she isn't.   She's taking   a bath.

A. Are they living   in Brooklyn?

B.   No,   they aren't. They're living   in Queens.

A. Are you washing   your shirt?

B.   No,   I'm not.   I'm washing   my jeans.

1. We're waiting for <u>the bus</u>.

   <u>What are you waiting for?</u>

2. He's thinking about <u>his girlfriend</u>.

   <u>Who is he thinking about?</u>

3. They're ironing <u>their shirts</u>.

   What are they ironing?

4. I'm calling <u>my landlord</u>.

   Who are you calling?

5. She's dancing with <u>her father</u>.

   Who is she dancing with?

6. He's watching <u>the news</u>.

   What is he watching?

7. They're complaining about <u>the rent</u>.

   What are they complaining about?

8. She's playing baseball with <u>her son</u>.

   Who is she playing with?

9. They're visiting <u>their cousins</u>.

   Who are they visiting?

10. We're looking at <u>the animals in the zoo</u>.

    What are you looking at?

11. I'm writing about <u>my favorite movie</u>.

    What are you writing about?

12. He's arguing with <u>his boss</u>.

    Who is he arguing with?

13. She's knitting a sweater for <u>her daughter</u>.

    Who is she knitting a sweater for?

14. We're making <u>pancakes</u>.

    What are you making pancakes?

15. I'm sending an e-mail to <u>my uncle</u>.

    Who are you sending an email to?

16. They're worrying about <u>their examination</u>.

    What are they worrying about?

17. She's talking to <u>the soccer coach</u>.

    Who's she talking about?

18. He's skating with <u>his grandparents</u>.

    Who's he skating with?

1. A. Where are you and your husband taking ____your____ children?

   B. ___We're___ taking ____them____ to the zoo.

2. A. Why is Richard calling all ____his____ friends today?

   B. ____He____ wants to tell ____them____ about ____his____ new car.

3. A. What are your parents going to give you for your birthday?

   B. I'm not sure, but ____they____ might give ____me____ a puppy.

4. A. Why is Susie visiting ____her____ grandparents?

   B. ____She____ wants to show ____them____ her new bicycle.

5. A. Why are you wearing a safety helmet on ____your____ head?

   B. ____I____ don't want to hurt ____my____ head while I'm skateboarding.

6. A. Where are you taking ____your____ new girlfriend on Saturday night?

   B. ____I'm____ taking ____her____ to see the new science fiction movie downtown.

7. A. Why are those students complaining about their teacher?

   B. ____They____ think she gives ____them____ too much homework.

8. A. Can I tell you and Dad about the party now?

   B. No. We're sleeping now. You can tell ____us____ about ____it____ tomorrow morning.

9. A. Why is Mrs. Jenkins waiting for the plumber?

   B. The sink is leaking. Charlie, the plumber, says ____he____ can fix ____it____.

10. A. Timmy, why are you arguing with ____your____ sister?

    B. ____She____ wants to play with ____my____ new toys, but she can't. They're mine.

L WHAT'S THE WORD?

1. You should never argue
   at
   to
   (with) a police officer.

2. We're watching
   at
   to
   (—) a game show on TV.

3. You shouldn't shout
   (at)
   to
   (—) people.

4. Do you write
   at
   (to)
   from your keypals very often?

5. They always complain
   at
   (—)
   (about) the weather.

6. We visit
   at
   to
   (—) our sister's friends in Texas once a year.

7. I'm helping
   at
   to
   (—) my neighbors
   to
   (with)
   (—) their garden.

8. I'm always frustrated when I have to wait
   (for)
   (—)
   at the bus.

9. Call
   to
   (—)
   at the exterminator right away!

Herbert (have) ___had__ 1 a very bad day yesterday. He usually gets up early, but yesterday

morning he (get up) _____ 2 very late! He (eat) _____ 3 breakfast quickly,

(rush) _____ 4 out of the house, and (run) _____ 5 to the bus stop. Unfortunately, he

(miss) _____ 6 the bus. He (wait) _____ 7 for ten minutes, but there weren't

any more buses, so he (decide) _____ 8 to walk to his office. Herbert was upset. He

(arrive) _____ 9 at work two and a half hours late!

Herbert (sit) _____ 10 down at his desk and (begin) _____ 11 his work. He

(call) _____ 12 a few people on the telephone, and he (type) _____ 13 a few letters.

But he was in a hurry, and he (make) _____ 14 a lot of mistakes. He (fix) _____ 15

the mistakes, but when he (finish) _____ 16 the letters and (put) _____ 17 them on

his desk, he (spill) _____ 18 water all over them.

At noon, Herbert (go) _____ 19 to the company cafeteria and (order) _____ 20 a

pizza for lunch. That was a big mistake. The pizza was very spicy, and Herbert (feel) _____ 21

sick for the rest of the day.

Herbert's afternoon was even worse than his morning. He (forget) _____ 22 about an

important meeting, his computer (crash) _____ 23, he (fall) _____ 24 asleep at his

desk, his chair (break) _____ 25, and he (hurt) _____ 26 his arm.

Herbert (leave) _____ 27 the office at 5:00, (take) _____ 28 the bus home, and

immediately (go) _____ 29 to bed! What a terrible, terrible day!

Listen and circle the correct answer.

1. yesterday ⟨every day⟩	4. yesterday / every day	7. yesterday / every day	10. yesterday / every day
2. ⟨yesterday⟩ every day	5. yesterday / every day	8. yesterday / every day	11. yesterday / every day
3. yesterday / every day	6. yesterday / every day	9. yesterday / every day	12. yesterday / every day

C **WHAT'S THE WORD?**

Fill in the missing words. Then read the story aloud.

decide	lift	need	paint	plant	roller-blade	wait	want

Last Saturday everyone __wanted__ 1 my help. In the morning, I _____ 2 heavy furniture for my wife, and I _____ 3 the bathroom walls. Then I _____ 4 in the park with my son and _____ 5 flowers with my daughter. In the afternoon, my brother _____ 6 my help. I went to a store with him and _____ 7 while he _____ 8 which suit to buy for his wedding.

D **PUZZLE:** *What Did They Do?*

Across
2. ride
3. teach
5. are
6. meet
7. deliver

Down
1. write
4. get
5. work

E   WHAT'S THE QUESTION?

1. _____Did you buy_____ the green one?   No, I didn't. I bought the blue one.

2. _____ a plane?   No, they didn't. They took a boat.

3. _____ a movie?   No, she didn't. She saw a play.

4. _____ French?   No, he didn't. He spoke Arabic.

5. _____ your arm?   No, I didn't. I broke my leg.

6. _____ at seven?   No, it didn't. It began at eight.

7. _____ to Paris?   No, she didn't. She flew to Rome.

8. _____ the beef?   No, we didn't. We had the chicken.

9. _____ with you?   No, they didn't. They went alone.

10. _____ too softly?   No, you didn't. You sang too loudly.

11. _____ your mother?   No, he didn't. He met my father.

12. _____ your keys?   No, I didn't. I lost my ring.

F   WHAT'S THE ANSWER?

was	were
wasn't	weren't

angry	hungry	prepared	scared	tired
bored	on time	sad	thirsty	

1. The students fell asleep in Professor Winter's class because _____they were bored_____.

2. I didn't finish my sandwich today because _____I wasn't hungry_____.

3. They went to bed early last night because _____they were tired._____.

4. She didn't do well on the test because _____she wasn't prepared._____.

5. He shouted at them because _____he was angry._____.

6. I missed the train this morning because _____I wasn't on time._____.

7. My daughter didn't finish all her milk because _____she wasn't thirsty_____.

8. I covered my eyes during the movie because _____I was scared_____.

9. They cried when they said good-bye at the airport because _____they were sad._____.

We went over 1-3. Go over again (handwritten)

1. Albert usually drives very carefully.

   He ___didn't drive___ carefully yesterday afternoon.

   He ___drove___ much too fast.

2. Alice usually comes home from work early.

   She _____ home early last night.

   She _____ home late.

3. I usually take the bus to work.

   I _____ the bus this morning.

   I _____ the train.

4. We usually go to the movies on Saturday.

   We _____ to the movies last Saturday.

   We _____ to a concert.

5. Carl and Tom usually forget their homework.

   They _____ their homework yesterday.

   They _____ their lunch.

6. Mr. Tyler usually wears a suit to the office.

   He _____ a suit today.

   He _____ jeans.

7. Professor Hall usually teaches biology.

   She _____ biology last semester.

   She _____ astronomy.

8. Mr. and Mrs. Miller usually eat dinner at 7:00.

   They _____ dinner at 7:00 last night.

   They _____ at 9:00.

9. My grandmother usually gives me a tie for my birthday.

   She _____ me a tie this year.

   She _____ me a watch.

10. Alan usually sits by himself in English class.

    He _____ by himself today.

    He _____ with all his friends.

11. I usually have cereal for breakfast.

    I _____ cereal this morning.

    I _____ eggs.

12. Amanda usually sings very beautifully.

    She _____ beautifully last night.

    She _____ very badly.

1. A. ____Did you____ clean your apartment this week?

   B. No, I ___didn't___ . I ___was___ too lazy.

2. A. ___Did you___ meet the company president at the office party?

   B. No, we ___didn't___ . But we ___met___ his wife.

3. A. ___Did___ Richard fall?

   B. Yes, he ___did___ . He skated very quickly, and he ___wasn't___ very careful.

4. A. ___Did___ Rita deliver all the pizzas today?

   B. No, ___she didn't___ . The people at 10 Main Street ___weren't___ home.

5. A. ___Did___ Roger ___fall___ asleep at the meeting this morning?

   B. No, ___he didn't___ . But he ___fell___ asleep later in his office. He ___was___ very tired.

6. A. ___Did___ you ride your motorcycle to work today?

   B. No, ___I didn't___ . I ___rode___ my bicycle, and I ___was___ late. My supervisor ___was___ upset.

7. A. _Did you_ like the movie?

   B. Yes, I _did_. It _was_ great! How about you? Did you like it?

   A. No, I _didn't_. I thought it _was_ boring.

8. A. _Was_ Mrs. Sanchez your Spanish teacher last semester?

   B. Yes, she _was_. _Were_ you in her class?

   A. No, _I wasn't_. I _didn't_ take Spanish. I took French.

9. A. _Did_ you complain to your landlord about the problems in your apartment?

   B. Yes, we _did_. He listened to us, but he _didn't_ fix anything. We _were_ very angry.

10. A. _Did_ the students dance gracefully in the school play?

    B. No, _they didn't_. They _danced_ very awkwardly. They _were_ very nervous.

11. A. Dad, _did_ you buy anything at the supermarket?

    B. Yes, _I did_. I _bought_ some food for dinner.

    A. _Did you_ buy any ice cream?

    B. Sorry. I _didn't_. There _wasn't_ any.

12. A. Grandpa, _were_ you a good soccer player when you _were_ young?

    B. Yes, _I was_. I _was_ a very good player. I _was_ fast, and I _wasn't_ clumsy.

I HOW DID IT HAPPEN?

1. How did Steven sprain his ankle? *(play tennis)*

   _____ He sprained his ankle while he was playing tennis. _____

2. How did your sister rip her pants? *(exercise)*

   _____

3. How did you break your arm? *(play volleyball)*

   _____

4. How did James poke himself in the eye? *(fix his sink)*

   _____

5. How did you and your brother hurt yourselves? *(skateboard)*

   _____

6. How did Mr. and Mrs. Davis trip and fall? *(dance)*

   _____

7. How did your father burn himself? *(cook french fries)*

   _____

8. How did your daughter get a black eye? *(fight with the kid across the street)*

   _____

9. How did you cut yourself? *(chop carrots)*

   _____

10. How did Robert lose his cell phone? *(jog in the park)*

    _____

11. How did you _____?

    _____

J GrammarRap: *What Did He Do?*

Listen. Then clap and practice.

A. What did he   do?

B. He did   his homework.

A. What did she   sing?

B. She sang   a song.

A. What did they   hide?

B. They hid   their money.

A. Where did you   go?

B. I went to   Hong Kong.

A. What did he   lose?

B. He lost his   watch.

A. What did he   study?

B. He studied   French.

A. What did it   cost?

B. It cost   a lot.

A. What did they   buy?

B. They bought   a wrench.

K GrammarRap: *I Was Talking to Bob When I Ran Into Sue*

Listen. Then clap and practice.

I was talking to   Bob when   I ran into   Sue.

I was waiting for   Jack when   I saw   Mary Lou.

They were cleaning   the house when   I knocked on the door.

He was dusting   a lamp when   it fell   on the floor.

She was learning to   drive when   I met her   last May.

She was buying   a car when   I saw her   today.

How	What	Where
How long	What kind of	Who
How many	When	Why

1. _____Who did you meet?_____ I met <u>the president</u>.

2. _____ She lost <u>her purse</u>.

3. _____ We did our exercises <u>at the beach</u>.

4. _____ They left <u>at 9:15</u>.

5. ___How get she get heare.___ She got here <u>by plane</u>.

6. _____ He sang <u>in a concert hall</u>.

7. _____ They stayed <u>for a week</u>.

8. ___what kind of movie did he saw.___ I saw a <u>science fiction</u> movie.

9. _____ He cried <u>because the movie was sad</u>.

10. _____ She wrote a letter to <u>her brother</u>.

11. _____ They complained about <u>the telephone bill</u>.

12. _____ We ate <u>a lot of</u> grapes.

13. _____ He spoke <u>at the meeting</u>.

14. _____ They lifted weights <u>all morning</u>.

15. _____ She gave a present to <u>her cousin</u>.

16. _____ I ordered <u>apple</u> pie.

17. _____ We rented <u>seven</u> videos.

18. _____ They sent an e-mail to <u>their teacher</u>.

19. _____ He fell asleep <u>during the lecture</u>.

20. _____ I lost my hat <u>while I was skiing</u>.

1. A. Did you go to Hong Kong?

   B. No, _____we didn't_____.

   A. Where _____did you go_____?

   B. _____We went_____ to Tokyo.

3. A. Did your flight to Japan leave on time?

   B. No, _____.

   A. How late _____

   _____?

   B. _____ two hours late.

5. A. Did you stay in a big hotel?

   B. No, _____.

   A. What kind of _____

   _____?

   B. _____.

2. A. Did you get there by boat?

   B. No, _____.

   A. How _____?

   B. _____.

4. A. Did you have good weather during the flight?

   B. No, _____.

   A. What kind of _____

   _____?

   B. _____ terrible weather.

6. A. Did you eat American food?

   B. No, _____.

   A. What kind of _____

   _____?

   B. _____.

(continued)

7. A. Did you take your camera with you?

B. No, _____.

A. What _____

_____?

B. _____ our camcorder.

9. A. Did you meet many Japanese?

B. No, _____.

A. Who _____?

B. _____ other tourists.

Where's the train station?

11. A. Did you speak Japanese?

B. No, _____.

A. What language _____

_____?

B. _____.

8. A. Did you get around the city by train?

B. No, _____.

A. How _____

_____?

B. _____.

10. A. Did you buy any clothing?

B. No, _____.

A. What _____?

B. _____ souvenirs.

12. A. Did you spend a lot of money?

B. Yes, _____.

A. How much _____

_____?

B. _____.

SOUND IT OUT!

Listen to each word and then say it.

this

1. chicken   3. river   5. busy
2. middle   4. kid   6. didn't

these

1. cheese   3. asleep   5. Steve
2. meat   4. receive   6. repeat

Listen and put a circle around the word that has the same sound.

1. clean: fine   middle   (these)
2. mix: ski   did   need
3. easy: Rita   break   eyes
4. video: machine   big   keep
5. east: build   little   green
6. symphony: mittens   life   retire
7. rip: knee   maybe   knit

Now make a sentence using all the words you circled, and read the sentence aloud.

8. _____ _____ _____ _____
   _____ _____

9. meat: Greek   Internet   eight
10. spill: healthy   his   rainy
11. promise: child   key   Richard
12. tea: every   men   into
13. cookie: with   speaks   bricks
14. milk: mine   advice   with
15. team: is   week   attractive
16. typical: sister   lazy   rebuild

Now make a sentence using all the words you circled, and read the sentence aloud.

17. _____ _____ _____ _____
    _____ _____

1. A. Did you ride your bicycle to work this morning?

    B. ___No, I didn't___ . I ___rode___ my

    motorcycle. ___I'm going to ride___ my bicycle to work tomorrow morning.

2. A. Did Tommy wear his new shoes to school today?

    B. __No, he didn't__ . He __wore__

    his old shoes. __He's going to wear__ his new shoes tomorrow.

3. A. Did Sally give her husband a sweater for his birthday this year?

    B. __No_____ . She __gave__

    him a tie. _____ him a sweater next year.

4. A. Did your parents drive to the mountains last weekend?

    B. ___No,_____ . They _____ to

    the beach. _____ going to drive to the mountains next weekend.

5. A. Did you and your family have eggs for breakfast this morning?

    B. ___No, we didn't___ . We ___had___

    pancakes. ___We are going___ eggs tomorrow morning.

6. A. Did you go out with Mandy last Saturday night?

    B. _____ . I _____

    out with Sandy. ___I am going to___ out with Mandy next Saturday night.

7. A. Did Howard write an interesting story for homework today?

    B. _____ . He _____ a

    boring one. _____ a more interesting story next time.

8. A. Did Shirley leave the office early this afternoon?

    B. _____ . She _____

    very late. _____ going to live early tomorrow afternoon.

BAD CONNECTIONS!

1. I'm really scared. Tomorrow my dentist is going to ###########.

   I'm sorry. I can't hear you. I think we have a bad connection. What's _your dentist going to do_?

2. We're very excited about our trip. We're going to go to ###########.

   What did you say? I can't hear you. Where _are you going to go_?

3. My son is very sad. His girlfriend is going to move to Alaska because #############.

   I'm sorry. We have a bad connection. Why _____ _____?

4. My parents are going to give me a ########### for my sixteenth birthday.

   Excuse me. I can't hear you. _____ _____?

5. I'm really nervous. I'm going to ########### for the first time tomorrow.

   We have a bad connection. _____ _____?

6. Please come to our wedding. We're going to get married next ###########.

   I'm sorry. I can't hear you. _____ _____?

7. I won't be home after school today. I'm going to meet ###########.

   This is a terrible connection! _____ _____?

(continued)

8.

I'm very excited! I'm going to name my new puppy ###########.

Sorry. I can't hear you.

_____

_____ ?

9.

I'm really upset. My parents are going to sell our house because ###########.

What did you say?

_____

_____ ?

10.

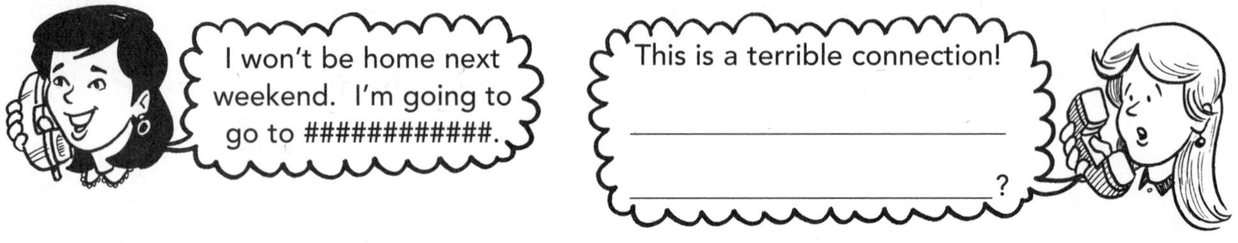

I won't be home next weekend. I'm going to go to ###########.

This is a terrible connection!

_____

_____ ?

11.

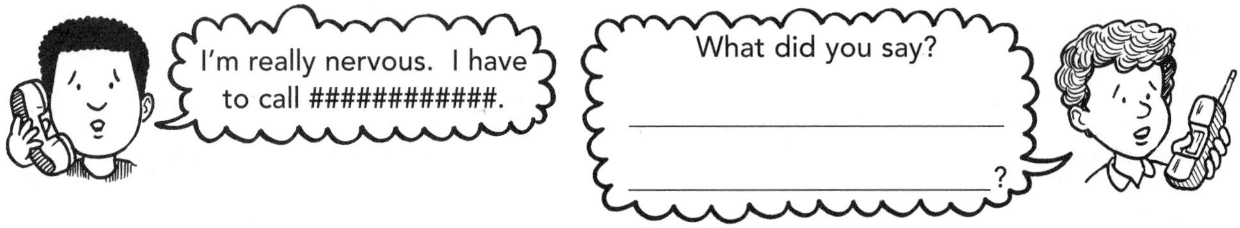

I'm really nervous. I have to call ###########.

What did you say?

_____

_____ ?

12.

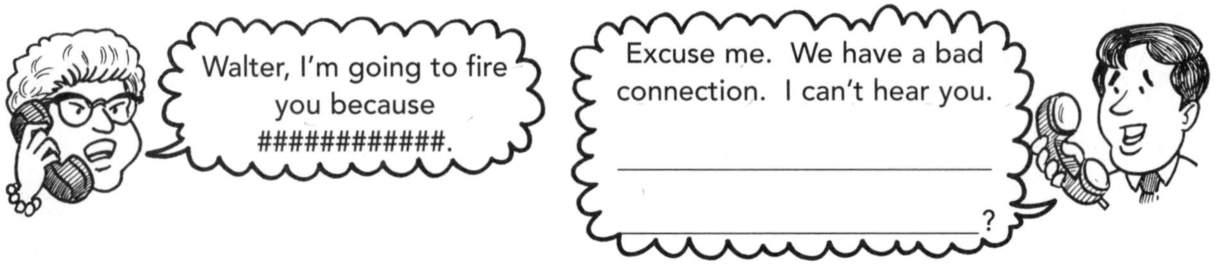

Walter, I'm going to fire you because ###########.

Excuse me. We have a bad connection. I can't hear you.

_____

_____ ?

C LISTENING

Listen and choose the time of the action.

1. a. last night
    (b.) tomorrow night

2. a. yesterday afternoon
    b. tomorrow afternoon

3. a. this weekend
    b. last weekend

4. a. this Saturday
    b. last Saturday

5. a. last week
    b. next week

6. a. yesterday evening
    b. this evening

7. a. tomorrow night
    b. last night

8. a. this weekend
    b. last weekend

9. a. this evening
    b. yesterday evening

10. a. last winter
    b. this winter

11. a. tomorrow morning
    b. yesterday morning

12. a. next semester
    b. last semester

James is a pessimist. He always thinks the worst will happen.

All his friends are optimists. They always tell James he shouldn't worry.

1. I'm afraid I ____won't have____ a good time at the office party tomorrow.

    Yes, ____you will____. ____You'll____ have a wonderful time.

2. I'm sure my son _____will hurt_____ himself in his soccer match today.

    No, ___he won't___. ___He won't___ hurt himself. He's always very careful.

3. I'm afraid my grandmother _____ get out of the hospital soon.

    Yes, _____. _____ get out of the hospital in a few days.

4. I'm afraid my wife _____ upset if I get a very short haircut.

    No, _____. _____ be upset.

5. I'm positive I _____ weight on my new diet.

    Yes, _____. _____ lose a lot of weight.

6. I'm afraid my children _____ my birthday this year.

    No, _____. _____ forget your birthday. They never forget it.

7. I'm afraid my landlord _____ our broken doorbell.

    Yes, _____. _____ fix it as soon as he can.

8. I'm afraid my new neighbors _____ like me.

    Of course _____. _____ you a lot. Everybody likes you.

9. I'm sure _____ catch a cold when we go camping this weekend.

    No, _____. _____ catch a cold, James. You worry too much!

attend	browse	clean	do	fill out	rain	watch	work out

1. A. Will Amanda be busy this afternoon?

   B. Yes, ___she will___.

      ___She'll be doing___ research at the library.

2. A. Will you be busy this evening?

   B. Yes, _____. _____

      _____ my income tax form.

3. A. Will Donald be home this afternoon?

   B. No, _____. _____

      _____ at his health club.

4. A. Will Mr. and Mrs. Lee be busy tonight?

   B. Yes, _____. _____

      _____ their apartment.

5. A. Will Grandpa be busy tonight?

   B. Yes, _____. _____

      _____ the web until after midnight.

6. A. Will you and your wife be home today?

   B. Yes, _____. _____

      _____ our favorite game show on TV.

7. A. Will Mom be home early tonight?

   B. No, _____. _____

      _____ a meeting.

8. A. Will the weather be nice this weekend?

   B. No, _____. _____

      _____ cats and dogs!

Pretend you're taking people on a tour of your city or town. Fill in the blanks with real places you know.

Good morning, everybody. This is _____ speaking. I'm so glad you'll be coming with me today on a tour of _____. We'll be leaving in just a few minutes.

First, I'll be taking you to see my favorite places in the city: _____, _____, and _____. Then we'll be going to _____ for lunch. In my opinion, this is the best restaurant in town. After that, I'll be taking you to see the other interesting tourist sights: _____, _____, and _____. This evening we'll be going to _____. _____. I'm sure you'll have a wonderful time.

G WHAT ARE THEY SAYING?

1. A. I'm sorry. I can't talk right now. I'm
      ___giving___ the kids a bath.

   B. How much longer _will you be giving_
      them a bath?

2. A. How much longer _____
      _____ your homework?

   B. I'll probably _____
      my homework for another half hour.

   A. Okay. I'll call you then.

3. A. Hi, Carol. This is Bob. Can you
      _____ for a minute?

   B. Sorry. I can't _____ right now.
      I'm _____ for a big test.

4. A. Sorry, Alan. I can't talk now. I'm
      _____ dinner with my family.

   B. How much longer _____
      _____ dinner?

Listen. Then clap and practice.

A.   Will you   be home   at a quarter   to three?

B.   Yes,   I will.   I'll be watching   TV.

A.   Will John   be home   at half   past two?

B.   Yes,   he will.   He'll be cooking   some stew.

A. Will your parents   be home   today   at four?

B.   Yes,   they will. They'll be washing   the floor.

A.   Will Jane   be home   if I call   at one?

B.   Yes,   she will.   She'll be feeding   her son.

A.   Will you   be home   at half   past eight?

B.   No,   I won't.   I'll be working   late.

A.   Will John   be home   at a quarter   to ten?

B.   No,   he won't.   He'll be visiting   a friend.

A. Will your parents   be home   tonight   at nine?

B.   No,   they won't. They'll be standing   in line.

A.   Will Jane   be home   if I call her   at seven?

B.   No,   she won't.   She'll be dancing   with Kevin.

WHOSE IS IT?

mine	his	hers	ours	yours	theirs

A. Hi, Robert. I found this wallet in my office today. Is it _____yours_____[1]?

B. No, it isn't _____[2], but it might be Tom's.

A. Maybe, but Tom hardly ever visits my office. It probably isn't _____[3].

B. It's small and blue. Maybe it's Martha's.

A. I asked her this morning. She says it isn't _____[4].

B. Is there anything inside the wallet?

A. There isn't any money, but there's a picture of three children.

B. It might belong to Mr. Hill. He and his wife have three children.

Maybe the children are _____[5].

A. I showed the picture to Mr. and Mrs. Hill. They said, "These

children aren't _____[6]. Our children are older."

B. Maybe you should give the wallet to our supervisor.

A. You know, it might be _____[7]. She has three children!

B. You're right. I'm positive it's _____[8]. I saw her children in her office last week.

J **GRAMMARRAP:** *Where's My Coat?*

Listen. Then clap and practice.

A. Where's my coat? I can't find mine.
Is this one mine or yours?

B. That one is mine. It isn't yours.
Yours is next to those doors.

A. Where's our umbrella? We can't find ours.
Is this one ours or theirs?

B. That one is theirs. It isn't yours.
Yours is under those chairs.

WHAT DOES IT MEAN?

Circle the correct answer.

1. Jim is wearing a tuxedo today.
   a. He's going to visit his grandmother.
   b. He's going to a wedding.
   c. He's going to work in a factory.

2. My brother has a black eye.
   a. He painted his eye.
   b. He's wearing dark glasses.
   c. He hurt his eye.

3. The teacher wasn't on time.
   a. She was early.
   b. She was late.
   c. She didn't have a good time.

4. They chatted online yesterday.
   a. They used a cell phone.
   b. They used a computer.
   c. They used a fax machine.

5. Everyone in my family is going to relax this weekend.
   a. We're going to rest this weekend.
   b. We're going to retire this weekend.
   c. We're going to return this weekend.

6. He wasn't prepared for his exam.
   a. He didn't study for the exam.
   b. He didn't take the exam.
   c. He was ready for the exam.

7. Could I ask you a favor?
   a. I want to help you.
   b. I want to give you something.
   c. I need your help.

8. It's a very emotional day for Janet.
   a. She's going to work.
   b. She's getting married.
   c. She's studying.

9. He's composing a symphony.
   a. He's writing a symphony.
   b. He's listening to a symphony.
   c. He's going to a concert.

10. George ripped his shirt.
    a. He has to wash his shirt.
    b. He has to iron his shirt.
    c. He has to sew his shirt.

11. Can I borrow your bicycle?
    a. I need your bicycle for a little while.
    b. I want to give you my bicycle.
    c. I want to buy your bicycle.

12. Every day I practice ballet.
    a. I sing every day.
    b. I play violin every day.
    c. I dance every day.

13. I'm going to lend my car to Bob today.
    a. Bob is going to drive my car.
    b. I'm going to drive Bob's car.
    c. Bob is going to give me his car.

14. Mr. and Mrs. Hansen love to talk about their grandchildren.
    a. They listen to them.
    b. They're very proud of them.
    c. They argue with them.

15. Rita did very well on her exam.
    a. She's happy.
    b. She's anxious.
    c. She's sad.

16. I'm going to repair my washing machine.
    a. I'm going to paint it.
    b. I'm going to fix it.
    c. I'm going to do laundry.

17. I need to assemble my new VCR.
    a. Can I borrow your screwdriver?
    b. Can I borrow your ladder?
    c. Can I borrow your TV?

18. I sprained my ankle.
    a. I broke my ankle.
    b. I hurt my ankle.
    c. I poked my ankle.

19. I'm going to fill out my income tax form.
  a. I'm going to return it.
  b. I'm going to read it.
  c. I'm going to answer the questions on the form.

20. They're playing Scrabble.
  a. They're playing a game.
  b. They're playing a sport.
  c. They're playing an instrument.

21. Mr. Smith is complaining to his boss.
  a. He's talking about his boss, and he's upset.
  b. He's talking to his boss, and he's happy.
  c. He's talking to his boss, and he's upset.

22. I'm going to call my wife right away.
  a. I'm going to call her immediately.
  b. I'm going to call her in a few hours.
  c. I'm going to call her when I have time.

23. My sister is an excellent athlete.
  a. She's an active person.
  b. She plays sports very well.
  c. She likes to watch sports.

24. My mother is looking forward to her retirement.
  a. She's happy about her new job.
  b. She wants to buy new tires for her car.
  c. Soon she won't have to go to work every day.

L LISTENING: *Looking Forward*

Listen to each story. Then answer the questions.

| *What Are Mr. and Mrs. Miller Looking Forward to?* | *What's Jonathan Looking Forward to?* | *What's Mrs. Grant Looking Forward to?* |

1. Mr. and Mrs. Miller _____ last week.
  (a.) moved
  b. relaxed
  c. flew to Los Angeles

2. Mr. and Mrs. Miller aren't going to _____ this weekend.
  a. repaint their living room
  b. assemble their VCR
  c. relax in their yard

3. They're going to _____ next weekend.
  a. assemble their computer
  b. relax
  c. paint flowers

4. Jonathan isn't _____ today.
  a. sitting in his office
  b. thinking about his work
  c. thinking about next weekend

5. Next weekend he'll be _____.
  a. working
  b. cooking and cleaning
  c. getting married

6. On their trip to Hawaii, Jonathan and his wife won't be _____.
  a. swimming in the ocean
  b. paying bills
  c. eating in restaurants

7. When she retires, Mrs. Grant will be _____.
  a. getting up early
  b. getting up late
  c. taking the bus to work

8. Mrs. Grant will _____ with her friends.
  a. go to museums
  b. work in her garden
  c. read books

9. She'll take her grandchildren to _____.
  a. the park and the beach
  b. the zoo and the beach
  c. the park and the zoo

A. Fill in the blanks.

Ex. Ann ___is___ a good skater, and

her children __skate__ well, too.

1. A. Mr. and Mrs. Lee _____
      wonderful dancers.

   B. I agree with you. They

      _____ very well.

2. A. Roger _____ very
      carelessly.

   B. I know. He's a terrible driver.

3. A. We don't swim very well.

   B. I disagree. I think _____

      excellent _____.

4. A. I type very well. I think _____

      a very good _____.

5. A. We _____ good _____,
      but we like to ski anyway.

B. Fill in the blanks.

1. A. Did you speak to Mrs. Baxter
      yesterday?

   B. No, I _____. I _____

      too busy. But I _____ to Mrs.
      Parker.

2. A. Did you buy juice when you were at
      the store?

   B. No, I _____. I forgot. But

      I _____ milk.

3. A. _____ they get up early this
      morning?

   B. No, they _____. They _____
      up very late.

4. A. Did Mr. Wong teach biology last
      semester?

   B. No, he _____. He _____
      astronomy because the astronomy

      teacher _____ sick all semester.

5. A. _____ you talk to Tom last night?

   B. No, I _____. I _____ to

      his wife. Tom _____ there when
      I called.

C. Write the questions.

Ex. We're arguing with <u>our landlord</u>.

   _____<u>Who are you arguing with?</u>_____

1. I'm writing about <u>my favorite movie</u>.

   _____

2. They're going to fix <u>their bookcase</u>.

   _____

3. He hiked <u>in the mountains</u>.

   _____

4. She'll be ready <u>in a few minutes</u>.

   _____

5. They arrived <u>by plane</u>.

   _____

6. We'll be staying until <u>Monday</u>.

   _____

7. She's going to hire <u>five</u> people.

   _____

D. Answer the questions.

Ex. What did your daughter do yesterday morning?

(do her homework) _____ She did her homework. _____

1. What's your sister doing today?

(adjust her satellite dish) _____

2. What does your brother do every evening?

(chat online) _____

3. What are you going to do next weekend?

(visit my mother-in-law) _____

4. What did Jack and Rick do yesterday afternoon?

(deliver groceries) _____

5. What was David doing when his children came home from school?

(bake a cake) _____

6. How will you get to work tomorrow?

(take the bus) _____

7. What will you and your husband be doing this evening?

(watch TV) _____

8. How did you cut your hand?

(chop carrots) _____

E. Listen to each question and then complete the answer.

Ex. Yes, _____ he does _____ .

1. Yes, _____ .

2. No, _____ .

3. Yes, _____ .

4. Yes, _____ .

5. No, _____ .

6. Yes, _____ .

7. No, _____ .

8. Yes, _____ .

1. I ride horses.

   ___I've ridden___ horses
   for many years.

2. I fly airplanes.

   _____ airplanes
   for several years.

3. I give injections at the
   hospital.

   _____ injections
   for many years.

4. I speak Italian.

   _____ it
   all my life.

5. I take photographs.

   _____ them
   for many years.

6. I do exercises every day.

   _____ them
   every day for many years.

7. I draw cartoons.

   _____ cartoons
   for several years.

8. I write for a newspaper.

   _____ for a
   newspaper for many years.

9. I drive carefully.

   _____ carefully
   all my life.

B **LISTENING**

Listen and choose the word you hear.

1. a. ridden
   b. written

2. a. taking
   b. taken

3. a. giving
   b. given

4. a. written
   b. driven

5. a. writing
   b. written

6. a. drawing
   b. doing

7. a. spoken
   b. speaking

8. a. done
   b. drawn

be	fly	give	ride	sing	take
draw	get ✓	go	see	swim	write

1. _____I've never flown_____
in a helicopter.

2. _____
a raise.

3. _____
in a limousine.

4. _____
a cartoon.

5. _____
a book.

6. _____
a trip to Hawaii.

7. _____
in a choir.

8. _____
in the Mediterranean.

9. _____
on television.

10. _____
on a cruise.

11. _____
a present to my teacher.

12. _____
a Broadway show.

D LISTENING

Is Speaker B answering Yes or No? Listen to each conversation and circle the correct answer.

1. (Yes)   No   3. Yes   No   5. Yes   No   7. Yes   No

2. Yes   No   4. Yes   No   6. Yes   No   8. Yes   No

fall	get	give	go	ride	wear

1. A. _____Have you ever gotten_____ stuck in bad traffic?

   B. Yes. As a matter of fact, _____I got_____ stuck in very bad traffic this morning.

2. A. _Have you ever ridden_ on a Ferris wheel?

   B. Yes, I have. _I rode_ on a Ferris wheel last weekend.

3. A. _Have you ever worn_ a tuxedo?

   B. Yes, I have. _I wore_ a tuxedo to my sister's wedding.

4. A. _Have you ever gone_ scuba diving?

   B. Yes, I have. _I went_ scuba diving last summer.

5. A. _Have you ever given_ blood?

   B. Yes, I have. _I gave_ blood a few months ago.

6. A. _Have you ever fallen_ on the sidewalk?

   B. Yes. In fact, _I fell_ on the sidewalk a few days ago.

F **GRAMMARRAP:** *Have You Ever?*

Listen. Then clap and practice.

A. Have you ever   seen   a rainbow?

    Have you ever   learned   to dance?

    Have you ever   flown   an airplane?

    Have you ever   gone   to France?

B. No, I've never   seen   a rainbow.

    I've never   learned   to dance.

    I've never   flown   an airplane.

    But I've often   gone   to France.

WHAT ARE THEY SAYING?

drive	eat	go	meet	see	speak	take	write

1. A. ___Have___ your children ___eaten___ breakfast yet?

   B. Yes, ___they have___. ___They ate___ breakfast a little while ago.

2. A. ___Has___ George ___driven___ his new car yet?

   B. Yes, ___he has___. ___He drove___ it for the first time this morning.

3. A. ___Has___ Gloria ___gone___ to the post office yet?

   B. Yes, ___she has___. ___She went___ to the post office a little while ago.

4. A. ___Have___ you and Jane ___seen___ the new movie at the Westville Mall?

   B. Yes, ___we have___. ___We saw___ it last Saturday night.

5. A. ___Have___ the employees ___taken___ inventory yet?

   B. Yes, ___they have___. ___They took___ inventory last weekend.

6. A. ___Have___ you ___spoken___ to the landlord yet?

   B. Yes, ___I have___. ___I spoke___ to him this morning.

7. A. ___Have___ I ___written___ a letter to the Carter Company yet?

   B. Yes, ___you have___. ___You wrote to___ them a letter last week.

8. A. ___Have___ you and your wife ___met___ your daughter's new boyfriend yet?

   B. Yes, ___we have___. ___We met___ him last Friday night.

1. Kenji and his girlfriend aren't going to eat at Burger Town today. __They've__ already __eaten__ at Burger Town this week. __They ate__ there on Monday.

2. My sister isn't going dancing tonight. __She's__ already __gone__ dancing this week. __She went__ dancing last night.

3. Timothy isn't going to wear his new jacket to work today. __He's__ already __worn__ it to work this week. __He wore__ it yesterday.

4. My husband and I aren't going to do our laundry today. __We've__ already __done__ our laundry this week. __We did__ it on Saturday.

5. Roger isn't going to give his girlfriend candy today. __He've__ already __given__ her candy this week. __He gave__ her candy yesterday morning.

6. I'm not going to see a movie today. __I've__ already __seen__ a movie this week. __I saw__ a movie on Wednesday.

7. We aren't going to buy fruit at the supermarket today. __We've__ already __bought fruit__ fruit at the supermarket this week. __We bought__ some fruit two days ago.

8. Susie isn't going to visit her grandparents today. __She's__ already __visited__ them this week. __She visited__ them yesterday.

9. David isn't going to take his children to the circus today. __He's__ already __taken__ them to the circus this week. __He took__ them to the circus a few days ago.

I WHAT'S THE WORD?

go / went / gone

1. We should ___go___ now.

2. They ___went___ home early today.

3. She's already ___gone___ home.

see / saw / seen

4. I've never ___seen___ him.

5. I ___saw___ her yesterday.

6. Do you ___see___ them often?

eat / ate / eaten

7. I _____ there this morning.

8. Has he ever _____ there?

9. Do you _____ there every day?

write / wrote / written

10. How often do you _____ to them?

11. She's already _____ her report.

12. He _____ her a very long letter.

wear / wore / worn

13. When will you _____ it?

14. He's never _____ it.

15. She _____ it today.

speak / spoke / spoken

16. Who _____ to you about it?

17. She can't _____ Chinese.

18. Have they _____ to you?

drive / drove / driven

19. They've never _____ there.

20. We never like to _____ there.

21. She _____ there today.

do / did / done

22. Did you _____ your homework?

23. We _____ that yesterday.

24. Have you ever _____ that?

WHAT ARE THEY SAYING?

1. A. Janet, you've got to do your homework.

   B. But, Mother, __I've__ already _____ my homework today.

   A. Really? When?

   B. Don't you remember? _____ my homework this afternoon.

   A. Oh, that's right. Also, _____ you _____ a letter to Grandma yet?

   B. Yes, _____. I wrote to her yesterday.

2. A. Would you like to swim at the health club tonight?

   B. I don't think so. _____ already _____ at the health club today.

   A. Really? When?

   B. _____ there this morning.

3. A. Are you going to take your vitamins?

   B. _____ already _____ them.

   A. Really? When?

   B. _____ them before breakfast.

   How about you? _____ you _____ yours?

   A. Yes, _____. I _____ mine when I got up.

4. A. I hope Jimmy gets a haircut soon.

   B. Don't worry, Mother. _____ already _____ one.

   A. I'm glad to hear that. When?

   B. _____ a haircut yesterday.

   A. That's wonderful!

5. A. When are you and Fred going to eat at the new restaurant downtown?

    B. _____ already _____ there.

    A. Really? When?

    B. _____ there last weekend.

    A. How was the food?

    B. It was terrible. It was the worst food we've ever _____!

6. A. When are you going to speak to the boss about a raise?

    B. _____ already _____ to her.

    A. Really? When?

    B. _____ to her this morning.

    A. What did she say?

    B. She said, "_____."

K **GRAMMARRAP:** *Have You Gone to the Bank?*

Listen. Then clap and practice.

A. Have you gone to the bank?

B.   Yes, I have.

    I went to the bank at noon.

A. Have they taken a vacation?

B.   Yes, they have.

    They took a vacation in June.

A. Has he written the letters?

B.   Yes, he has.

    He wrote the letters today.

A. Has she gotten a raise?

B.   Yes, she has.

    She got a raise last May.

buy	dance	fly	go	read	see	swim
clean	eat	give	make	ride	study	take

1. A. What's the matter, Susan? You aren't riding very well today.

   B. I know. _____I haven't ridden_____ in a long time.

2. A. I can't believe it! These cars are very expensive.

   B. Remember, we _____ a new car in a long time.

3. A. Are you nervous?

   B. Yes, I am. _____ in an airplane in a long time.

4. A. Are you excited about your vacation?

   B. Yes, I am. _____ a vacation in a long time.

5. A. You aren't swimming very well today.

   B. I know. _____ in a long time.

6. A. Buster is really hungry.

   B. I know. He _____ anything in a long time.

7. A. Susie's room is very dirty.

   B. I know. She _____ it in a long time.

8. A. I think Timmy watches too much TV.

   B. You're right. _____ a book in a long time.

9. A. Mom, who was the sixteenth
   president of the United States?

   B. I'm not sure. _____
   American history in a long time.

11. A. Are you nervous?

    B. Yes, I am. _____
    blood in a long time.

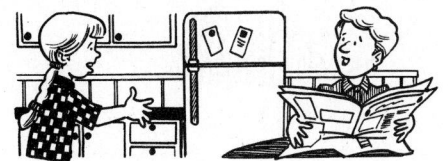

13. A. Is there any fruit in the refrigerator?

    B. No, there isn't. I _____
    to the supermarket in a long time.

10. A. Everyone says the new movie at the
    Center Cinema is excellent.

    B. Let's see it. We _____
    a good movie in a long time.

12. A. What's Dad doing?

    B. He's making dinner. _____
    dinner in a long time.

14. A. Ouch!!

    B. Sorry. _____
    in a long time.

M PUZZLE: *What Have They Already Done?*

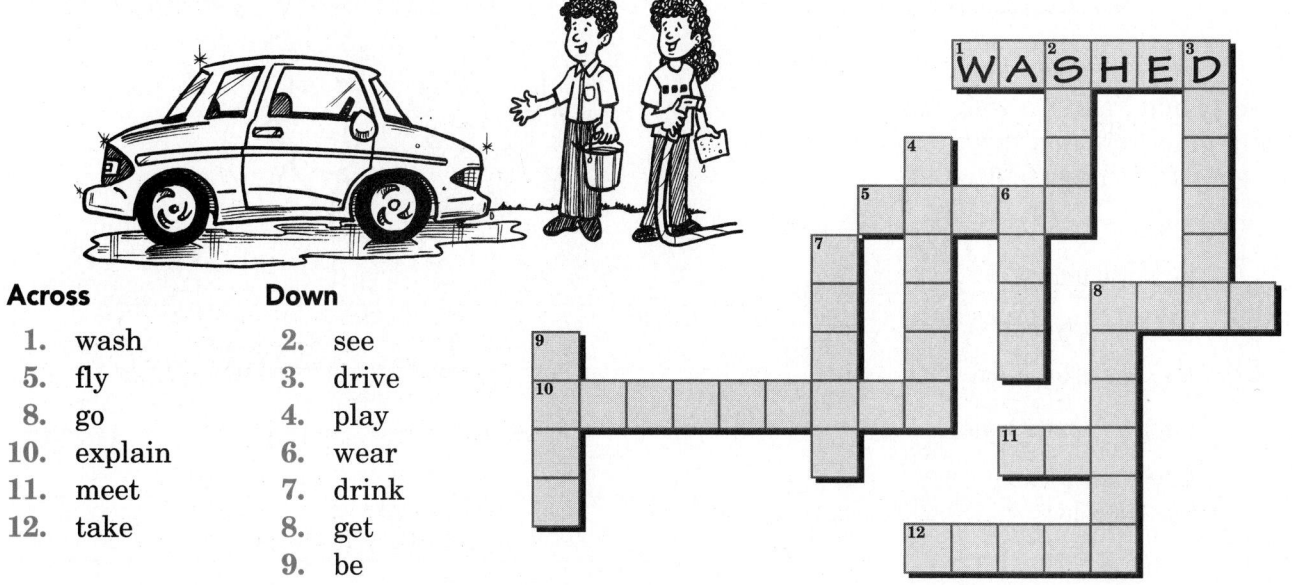

Across

1. wash
5. fly
8. go
10. explain
11. meet
12. take

Down

2. see
3. drive
4. play
6. wear
7. drink
8. get
9. be

Richard is going to have a party tonight, and he has a lot of things to do.

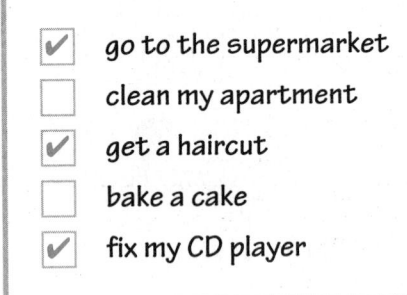

✔	go to the supermarket
	clean my apartment
✔	get a haircut
	bake a cake
✔	fix my CD player

1. _____ He's already gone to the supermarket.

2. _____ He hasn't cleaned his apartment yet.

3. _____

4. _____

5. _____

Susan is going to work this morning, and she has a lot of things to do.

✔	take a shower
	do my exercises
	feed the cat
✔	walk the dog
	eat breakfast

6. _____

7. _____

8. _____

9. _____

10. _____

Beverly and Paul are going on a trip tomorrow, and they have a lot of things to do.

	do our laundry
✔	get our paychecks
✔	pay our bills
	pack our suitcases
	say good-bye to our friends

11. _____

12. _____

13. _____

14. _____

15. _____

Roberta is very busy today. She has a lot of things to do at the office.

✔	write to Mrs. Lane
✔	call Mr. Sanchez
☐	meet with Ms. Wong
☐	read my e-mail
✔	send a fax to the Ace Company

16. _____

17. _____

18. _____

19. _____

20. _____

You have a lot of things to do today. What have you done? What haven't you done?

1. ....

2. ....

3. ....

4. ....

5. ....

0 LISTENING

What things have these people done? What haven't they done? Listen and check *Yes* or *No*.

		Yes	No			Yes	No
1.	do homework	✔	____	5.	do the laundry	____	____
	practice the violin	____	✔		vacuum the rugs	____	____
2.	write the report	____	____	6.	get the food	____	____
	send a fax	____	____		clean the house	____	____
3.	feed the dog	____	____	7.	speak to the landlord	____	____
	eat breakfast	____	____		call Ajax Electric	____	____
4.	fix the pipes	____	____	8.	hook up the VCR	____	____
	repair the washing machine	____	____		read the instructions	____	____

1. A. Have you spoken to David recently?

   B. Yes, I __have__. I _____ to him last night.

   A. What _____ he say?

   B. He's worried because he's going to fly in a helicopter this week, and he's never _____ in a helicopter before.

2. A. _____ you seen any good movies recently?

   B. No, I _____. I _____ a movie last week, but it was terrible.

   A. Really? What movie did you _____?

   B. *The Man from Madagascar.* It's one of the worst movies I've ever _____.

3. A. I think I forgot to do something, but I can't remember what I forgot to do.

   B. Have you _____ the mail to the post office?

   A. Yes. I _____ it to the post office an hour ago.

   B. _____ you _____ a fax to the Ace Company?

   A. Yes. I _____ them a fax this morning.

   B. _____ you _____ the employees their paychecks?

   A. Uh-oh! That's what I forgot to do!

4. A. _____ you gone on vacation yet?

   B. Yes, I _____. I _____ to Venice. It was phenomenal!

   A. _____ you ever _____ to Venice before?

   B. Yes, I _____. I _____ there a few years ago.

5. A. What _____ you get for your birthday?

B. My family _____ me seventy-five dollars.

A. That's fantastic! What _____?

B. Going to buy? I've already _____ all my birthday money.

A. Really? What _____ buy?

B. I _____ a lot of CDs. Do you want to _____ to them?

6. A. Are you ready to leave soon?

B. No, _____. I haven't _____ a shower yet.

A. But you _____ up an hour ago. You're really slow today. _____ you eaten breakfast yet?

B. Of course _____. I _____ a little while ago, and I've already _____ the dishes.

A. Well, hurry up! It's 8:30. I don't want to be late.

Q LISTENING

Listen to each word and then say it.

1. job
2. jacket
3. juice
4. jam
5. jog
6. pajamas
7. journalist
8. just
9. Jennifer

10. you
11. yoga
12. yellow
13. yard
14. yesterday
15. young
16. yogurt
17. yet
18. New York

Julia's keyboard is broken. The j's and the y's don't always work. Fill in the missing j's and y's and then read Julia's letters aloud.

1.

___J__udy,

Have you seen my blue and ___y__ellow ___j__acket at ___our house? I think I left it there ___esterday after the ___azz concert. I've looked everywhere, and I ___ust can't find it anywhere.

___ulia

2.

Dear ___ennifer,

We're sorry ___ou haven't been able to visit us this ___ear. Do ___ou think ___ou could come in ___une or ___uly? We really en___oyed ___our visit last ___ear. We really want to see ___ou again.

___ulia

3.

___eff,

___ack and I have gone out ___ogging, but we'll be back in ___ust a few minutes. Make ___ourself comfortable. ___ou can wait for us in the ___ard. We haven't eaten lunch ___et. We'll have some ___ogurt and orange ___uice when we get back.

___ulia

4.

Dear ___ane,

We ___ust received the beautiful pa___amas ___ou sent to ___immy. Thank ___ou very much. ___immy is too ___oung to write to ___ou himself, but he says "Thank ___ou." He's already worn the pa___amas, and he's en___oying them a lot.

___ulia

5.

Dear ___anet,

___ack and I are coming to visit ___ou and ___ohn in New ___ork. We've been to New ___ork before, but we haven't visited the Statue of Liberty or the Empire State Building ___et. See ___ou in ___anuary or maybe in ___une.

___ulia

6.

Dear ___oe,

We got a letter from ___ames last week. He has en___oyed college a lot this ___ear. His favorite sub___ects are German and ___apanese. He's looking for a ___ob as a ___ournalist in ___apan, but he hasn't found one ___et.

___ulia

1. He's already eaten lunch.

   _____ is

   __✔__ has

2. He's eating lunch.

   __✔__ is

   _____ has

3. She's taking a bath.

   _____ is

   _____ has

4. She's taken a bath.

   _____ is

   _____ has

5. He's having a good time.

   _____ is

   _____ has

6. She's going to get up.

   _____ is

   _____ has

7. He's bought a lot of CDs recently.

   _____ is

   _____ has

8. It's snowing.

   _____ is

   _____ has

9. She's thirsty.

   _____ is

   _____ has

10. He's got to leave now.

    _____ is

    _____ has

11. Where's the nearest health club?

    _____ is

    _____ has

12. She's written the report.

    _____ is

    _____ has

13. He's taking a lot of photographs.

    _____ is

    _____ has

14. He's taken a few photographs.

    _____ is

    _____ has

15. He's spent all his money.

    _____ is

    _____ has

16. There's a library across the street.

    _____ is

    _____ has

17. She's gone kayaking.

    _____ is

    _____ has

18. It's very warm.

    _____ is

    _____ has

19. He's embarrassed.

    _____ is

    _____ has

20. This is the best book she's ever read.

    _____ is

    _____ has

for   since

1. How long have you had a headache?

__I've had a headache__

__since__ this morning.

2. How long have your parents been married?

They been married *for* _____ a long time.

3. How long has your brother owned a motorcycle?

_____ *since* _____ last summer.

4. How long has your sister been interested in astronomy?

_____ *for* _____ several years.

5. How long have you had a cell phone?

_____ *since* _____ last month.

6. How long have you and your husband known each other?

_____ *since* _____ 1994.

7. How long have the Wilsons had a dog?

_____ *for* _____ a few weeks.

8. How long have you had problems with your upstairs neighbor?

_____ *for* _____ a year.

9. How long has your daughter been a computer programmer?

_____ *since* _____ 2000.

10. How long has your son played in the school orchestra?

_____ *since* _____ September.

11. How long have there been mice in your attic?

_____ *for* _____ two months.

1. ___How long has___ your daughter ___wanted to be an engineer___ ?

   She's wanted to be an engineer for a long time.

2. ___How long has___ James ___owned his own house___ ?

   He's owned his own house since 2001.

3. ___How long have___ your grandparents ___been married___ ?

   They've been married for 50 years.

4. ___How long have___ you ___been interested in photography___ ?

   I've been interested in photography since last year.

5. ___How long has___ Gregory ___worn glasses___ ?

   He's worn glasses since last spring.

6. ___How long have___ your cousins ___known how to snowboard___ ?

   They've known how to snowboard for a few years.

7. ___How long has___ your son ___has a girlfriend___ ?

   He's had a girlfriend for several months.

8. ___How long has___ there ___been a pizza shop in town___ ?

   There's been a pizza shop in town since last fall.

C **GrammarRap:** *How Long Have You Known Maria?*

Listen. Then clap and practice.

A. How long have you   known   Maria?

B. I've known her   since I was   two.

A. Have you met   her older   sister?

B. No, I haven't.   Have you?

A. How long   has your son   been in college?

B. He's been there   since early   September.

A. Does he like   all of his   courses?

B. I think so.   I can't   remember.

A. How long have   your friends   lived in London?

B. They've lived there   since two thousand   one.

A. Have you visited them   since they   moved there?

B. Yes, I have.   It was fun.

A. How long has   your brother   been married?

B. He's been married   for seven   months.

A. Have you seen him   since   his wedding?

B. I've seen him   only   once.

54   Activity Workbook

1. _____I'm_____ sick today.

   ___I've been sick___ since I got up this morning.

3. Roger _____ how to ski.

   _____ how to ski since he took lessons last winter.

5. _____ lost.

   _____ lost since we arrived here this morning.

7. _____ cold and cloudy.

   _____ cold and cloudy since we got here last weekend.

9. My boyfriend _____ bored.

   _____ bored since the concert began forty-five minutes ago.

2. Rita _____ a swollen knee.

   _____ a swollen knee since she played soccer last Saturday.

4. _____ nervous.

   _____ nervous since they got married a few hours ago.

6. I _____ a stiff neck.

   _____ a stiff neck since I went to a tennis match yesterday.

8. My daughter _____ the cello.

   _____ played the cello since she was six years old.

10. _____ afraid of dogs.

    _____ afraid of dogs since my neighbor's dog bit me last year.

Listen and choose the correct answer.

1. a. Bob is in the army.
   b. Bob is engaged. *(circled)*

2. a. Carol is in music school.
   b. Carol is a professional musician.

3. a. Michael has been home for a week.
   b. Michael hurt himself this week.

4. a. She hasn't started her new job.
   b. She gets up early every morning.

5. a. Richard is in college.
   b. Richard hasn't eaten in the cafeteria.

6. a. Nancy and Tom met five and a half years ago.
   b. Nancy and Tom met when they were five and a half years old.

7. a. They play soccer every weekend.
   b. They're eight years old.

8. a. Patty is a teenager.
   b. Patty has short hair.

9. a. Ron used to own his own business.
   b. Ron moved nine years ago.

10. a. She's interested in astronomy.
    b. She's eleven years old.

11. a. He's in high school.
    b. He isn't in high school now.

12. a. Alan has owned his house for fifteen years.
    b. Alan doesn't have problems with his house now.

F CROSSWORD

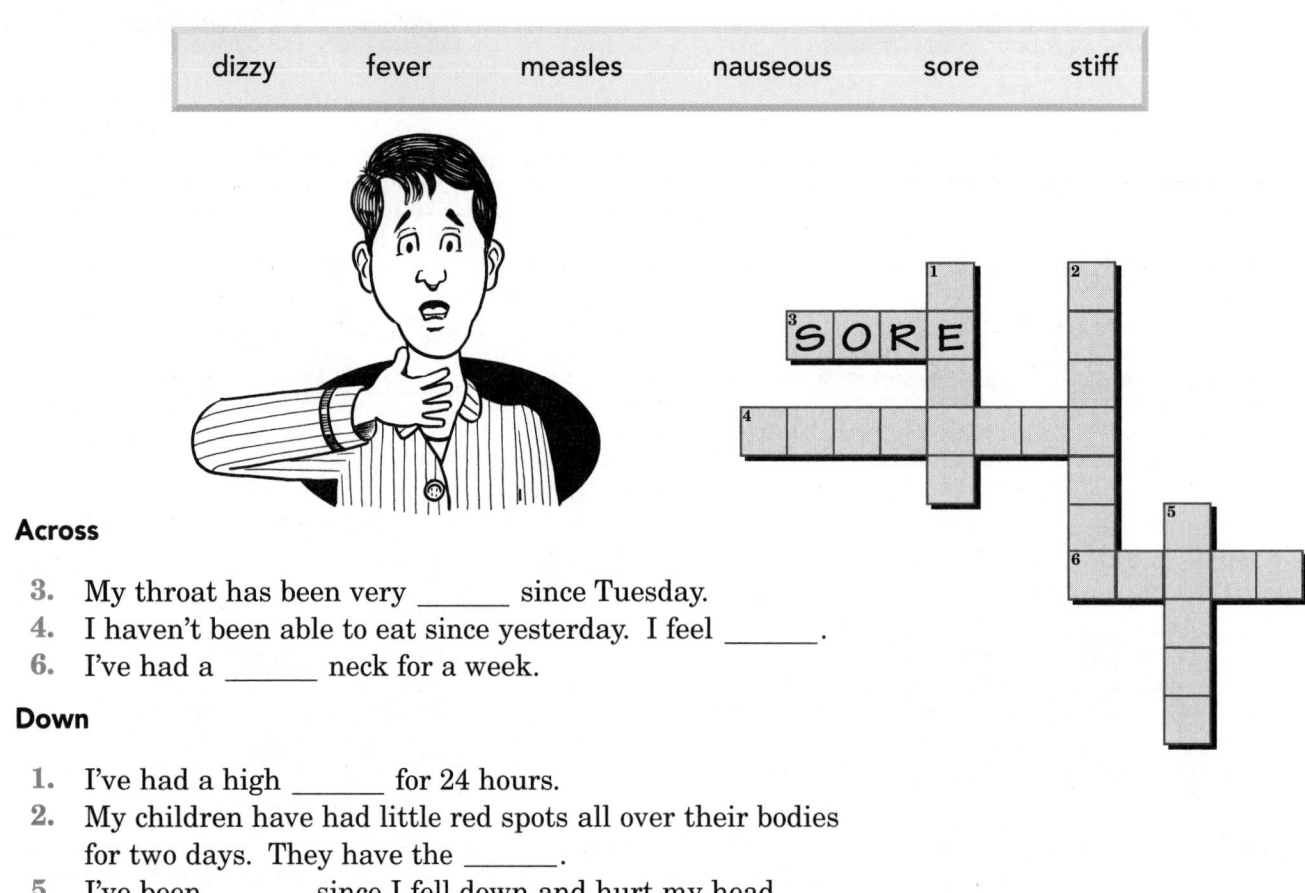

| dizzy | fever | measles | nauseous | sore | stiff |

Across

3. My throat has been very _____ since Tuesday.
4. I haven't been able to eat since yesterday. I feel _____.
6. I've had a _____ neck for a week.

Down

1. I've had a high _____ for 24 hours.
2. My children have had little red spots all over their bodies for two days. They have the _____.
5. I've been _____ since I fell down and hurt my head.

G SCRAMBLED SENTENCES

Unscramble the sentences.

1. she   a   jazz   Julie   liked   teenager.   has   was   since

   _____ Julie has liked jazz since she was a teenager. _____

2. he   play   little   the   since   known   a   boy.   He's   piano   was   how   to

   _____

3. since   I've   was   in   I   astronomy   young.   interested   been

   _____

4. since   been   they   college.   engaged   They've   finished

   _____

5. been   he   a   cooking   He's   graduated   from   chef   school.   since

   _____

6. she   wanted   be   to   teacher   eighteen   She's   a   years   since   old.   was

   _____

7. moved   ago.   business   They've   their   year   owned   since   a   they   here   own

   _____

H WRITE ABOUT YOURSELF

1. I'm interested in _____ .

   I've been interested in _____ since _____ .

2. I own _____ .

   I've owned _____ since _____ .

3. I like _____ .

   I've _____ since _____ .

4. I want to _____ .

   I've _____ since _____ .

5. I know how to _____ .

   I've _____ since _____ .

be	have	speak	teach	visit	walk

1. Mr. and Mrs. Miller __walk__ every day.

   _____ every day since Mr. Miller had problems with his heart last

   year. Before that, _____ never

   _____. They stayed home and watched TV.

2. Sam _____ with a Boston accent.

   _____ with a Boston accent since he moved to Boston last summer.

   Before that, _____ with a New York accent.

3. Terry _____ a truck driver. She drives a truck between the east coast

   and the west coast. _____ a truck driver for a year. Before that,

   _____ a taxi driver.

4. Before he moved to Brazil, Professor Baker

   _____ French. Now _____

   English. _____ English at a Brazilian university for the past two years.

5. Your Uncle Walter _____ already

   _____ us five times this year!

   Last year, he _____ us only twice. How many times will he

   _____ us next year?!

6. Tiffany _____ long blonde hair.

   _____ long blonde hair since she became a movie star. Before that, she

   _____ short brown hair. Tiffany looks very different now!

Victor
(be)

| musician | 1990–now |
| photographer | 1982–1989 |

1. How long ___has Victor been___ a musician?

   ___He's been a musician___ since ___1990___.

2. How long ___was he___ a photographer?

   ___He was a photographer___ for ___7 years___.

Mrs. Sanchez
(teach)

| science | 1995–now |
| math | 1985–1994 |

3. How long _____ science?

   _____ since _____.

4. How long _____ math?

   _____ for _____.

my grandparents
(have)

| dog | 1998–now |
| cat | 1986–1997 |

5. How long _____ a cat?

   _____ for _____.

6. How long _____ a dog?

   _____ since _____.

Betty
(work)

| bank | 2000–now |
| mall | 1997–1999 |

7. How long _____ at the bank?

   _____ since _____.

8. How long _____ at the mall?

   _____ for _____.

my parents
(live)

| Miami | 2001–now |
| New York | 1980–2000 |

9. How long _____ in New York?

   _____ for _____.

10. How long _____ in Miami?

    _____ since _____.

1. Do you still go skiing every winter?

   No. ....
   .... (for/since) ....
   ....

2. Do you still live .... ?

   No. ....
   .... (for/since) ....
   ....

3. Are you still a/an .... ?

   No. ....
   .... (for/since) ....
   ....

4. How long have you been interested in .... ?

   ....
   .... (for/since) ....
   ....

5. Do you still .... in your free time?

   No. ....
   .... (for/since) ....
   ....

6. Do your brothers still call you "Tiny Tim"?

No. ....
.... (for/since) ....
....

7. How long have you ....
....
.... ?

....
.... (for/since) ....
....

8. Do you still ....
....
.... ?

No. ....
.... (for/since) ....
....

L LISTENING

Listen and choose the correct answer.

1. a. He's always been a salesperson.
    (b.) He was a cashier.

2. a. His daughter was in medical school.
    b. His daughter is in medical school.

3. a. Her parents haven't always lived in a house.
    b. Her parents have always lived in a house.

4. a. He's always wanted to be an actor.
    b. He isn't in college now.

5. a. They exercise at their health club every day.
    b. They haven't exercised at their health club since last year.

6. a. James hasn't always been a bachelor.
    b. James has been married for ten years.

7. a. Jane has wanted to meet a writer.
    b. Jane wants to be a writer.

8. a. He's never broken his ankle.
    b. He's never sprained his ankle.

9. a. She's always liked rock music.
    b. She hasn't always liked classical music.

10. a. Billy has had a fever for two days.
    b. Billy has had a sore throat for two days.

11. a. Jennifer has always been the manager.
    b. Jennifer hasn't been a salesperson since last fall.

12. a. He's interested in modern art now.
    b. He's always been interested in art.

WHAT'S THE WORD?

for	since

1. We've been living here __since__ 2001.

2. It's been raining _____ two days.

3. I've been listening to this CD _____ an hour.

4. She's been flying airplanes _____ 1995.

5. Billy, you've been roller-blading _____ this morning!

6. He's been practicing the cello _____ three and a half hours.

7. Our neighbors have been vacuuming _____ 7 A.M.

8. We've been having problems with our heat _____ a week.

B **CHOOSE**

1. I've been working here since _____.
   a. last month
   b. three months

2. He's been taking a shower for _____.
   a. this afternoon
   b. half an hour

3. It's been ringing for _____.
   a. two o'clock
   b. a few minutes

4. She's been studying since _____.
   a. eight o'clock
   b. an hour

5. They've been dating for _____.
   a. high school
   b. six months

6. I've been feeling sick since _____.
   a. twelve hours
   b. yesterday

1. How long have you been studying?

I've been studying since early this morning.

2. How long has Ann been feeling sick?

_____ a few days.

3. How long has Tom been having problems with his car?

_____ a week.

4. How long have the people next door been arguing?

_____ last night.

5. How long have we been waiting?

_____ forty-five minutes.

6. How long has that cell phone been ringing?

_____ the play began.

7. How long has Professor Drake been talking?

_____ an hour and a half.

8. How long have Rick and Sally been dating?

_____ high school.

9. How long have you been teaching?

_____ 1975.

10. How long have I been chatting online?

_____ more than two hours.

D WHAT ARE THEY DOING?

| assemble | bake | bark | browse | do | jog | look | make | plant |

1. Larry ____is looking____ for his keys.

____He's been looking____ for his keys all morning.

2. My sister _____ in the park.

_____ in the park since 8 A.M.

3. The dog next door _____.

_____ all day.

4. Our neighbors _____ flowers.

_____ flowers for several hours.

5. Michael _____ his homework.

_____ his homework since dinner.

6. My wife _____ the web.

_____ the web for an hour.

7. Mr. and Mrs. Lee _____ their son's new bicycle.

_____ it all afternoon.

8. I'm _____ cookies.

_____ cookies since two o'clock.

9. You and your brother _____ a lot of noise!

_____ noise since you got up.

E LISTENING

Listen and choose the correct time expressions to complete the sentences.

1. (a.) 1995.
   b. a few years.

2. a. 1:45.
   b. forty-five minutes.

3. a. 3 o'clock.
   b. thirty minutes.

4. a. yesterday.
   b. several days.

5. a. 7:30 this morning.
   b. more than an hour.

6. a. 7 o'clock.
   b. a half hour.

7. a. a few weeks.
   b. last month.

8. a. about three hours.
   b. 4 o'clock.

9. a. early this morning.
   b. twenty minutes.

F 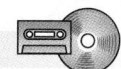 **GRAMMARRAP:** *How Long?*

Listen. Then clap and practice.

A.　　　　How long have you been　working　　　at the mall?

B.　　I've been working　　　at the mall　　　since the fall.

A.　　　　How long has she been　wearing　　　her new ring?

B.　She's been wearing　　　her new ring　　since the spring.

A.　　　　How long have you been　living　　　　in L.A.?

B.　We've been living　　　　in L.A.　　　since May.

A.　　　　How long has he been　waiting　　　for the train?

B.　He's been waiting　　since it started　　　to rain.

A.　　　　How long have you been　looking for　　that mouse?

B.　We've been looking　　since we rented　　　this house.

make	play	run	snow	study	take	vacuum	wait	wear	work

1. Excuse me.

   <u>Have you been waiting</u> in line for a long time?

   Yes, I <u>have</u>.

   <u>I've been waiting</u> for more than an hour.

2. What a terrible day!

   _____ for a long time?

   Yes, _____

   since early this morning.

3. Your son plays the violin very beautifully.

   _____ lessons for a long time?

   Yes, _____

   lessons since he was five.

4. _____ here for a long time?

   No, _____

   I've _____ here for only a week.

5. _____ your car _____ strange noises for a long time?

   Yes, _____

   these noises all week.

6. You look tired.

   _____ for a long time?

   Yes, _____

   all morning.

7. Your children speak French very well.

_____ it for a long time?

Yes, _____.

_____ French for six years.

8. I'm really tired.

_____ for a long time?

Yes, we _____.

_____ since 6 A.M.

9. Your pants are dirty.

_____ them all week?

No, _____.

_____ them for only a few hours.

10. This is the sixth game you've won today.

_____ for a long time?

No, _____.

_____ for only a few months.

H LISTENING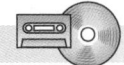

Listen and choose what the people are talking about.

1. (a.) traffic
   b. a computer

2. a. a wall
   b. the furniture

3. a. the guitar
   b. my bills

4. a. the drums
   b. tennis

5. a. the cookies
   b. the babies

6. a. the cake
   b. the bridge

7. a. her composition
   b. her bicycle

8. a. books
   b. trains

9. a. a sandwich
   b. a novel

10. a. socks
    b. chairs

11. a. the president
    b. CDs

12. a. a restaurant
    b. a neighbor

13. a. fruit
    b. my car

14. a. a test
    b. a cake

15. a. videos
    b. problems

1 SOUND IT OUT!

Listen to each word and then say it.

	this				these

1. b<u>i</u>lls 3. ch<u>i</u>cken 5. b<u>ui</u>lding 6. <u>i</u>tself

2. off<u>i</u>cer 4. t<u>i</u>cket

1. w<u>ee</u>k 3. br<u>ie</u>fcase 5. f<u>e</u>ver

2. sp<u>ea</u>k 4. friendl<u>y</u> 6. <u>ea</u>ten

Listen and put a circle around the word that has the same sound.

1. th<u>i</u>n: pol<u>i</u>ce   t<u>i</u>red   (<u>i</u>nterested)

2. b<u>ui</u>ld: h<u>ea</u>dache   <u>i</u>s   sw<u>ea</u>ter

3. r<u>ea</u>d: St<u>e</u>ve's   b<u>ee</u>n   tr<u>y</u>

4. <u>i</u>f: <u>i</u>n   b<u>i</u>te   tax<u>i</u>

5. l<u>i</u>ve: m<u>e</u>t   h<u>i</u>story   ch<u>i</u>ld

6. f<u>i</u>shing: sc<u>i</u>ence   wr<u>i</u>ting   s<u>i</u>ster

7. p<u>ie</u>ce: ver<u>y</u>   w<u>ea</u>r   w<u>i</u>nter

8. <u>ea</u>st: h<u>i</u>re   Chin<u>e</u>se   r<u>ea</u>dy

Now make a sentence using all the words you circled, and read the sentence aloud.

9. ....

10. k<u>ey</u>:   d<u>i</u>nner   rec<u>ei</u>ve   th<u>i</u>nk

11. tenn<u>i</u>s: <u>ea</u>sy   h<u>ea</u>ter   th<u>i</u>s

12. complet<u>e</u>: an<u>y</u>   g<u>e</u>t   tr<u>y</u>

13. k<u>ee</u>p: b<u>u</u>sy   P<u>e</u>ter   d<u>i</u>sturb

14. tux<u>e</u>do: t<u>y</u>pe   <u>i</u>f   w<u>ee</u>k

15. L<u>i</u>nda: d<u>i</u>dn't   gr<u>ee</u>n   br<u>i</u>ght

16. m<u>ee</u>ting: ch<u>i</u>ld   forg<u>e</u>t   <u>e</u>-mail

Now make a sentence using all the words you circled, and read the sentence aloud.

17. ....

YOU DECIDE: *What Have They Been Doing?*

1.

I have a sore throat.

No wonder you have a sore throat!

You've been singing all day.

2.

My back hurts.

No wonder your back hurts!

all day.

3.

Bob has a terrible sunburn.

No wonder he has a terrible sunburn!

all day.

4.

Nancy is very tired.

No wonder she's very tired!

all day.

5.

Jane and I have headaches.

No wonder you have headaches!

all day.

6.

Bob and Judy are very disappointed.

No wonder they're very disappointed!

all day.

7.

I can't finish my dinner.

No wonder you can't finish your dinner!

all day.

8.

Victor doesn't have any money.

No wonder he doesn't have any money!

all day.

| complain | eat | go | make | read | see | study | swim | talk | write |

1. My husband and I are very full. <u>We've been eating</u> for the past two hours. <u>We've</u> already <u>eaten</u> soup, salad, chicken, and vegetables. And our dinner isn't finished.

<u>We haven't eaten</u> our dessert yet!

2. Dr. Davis is tired. _____ patients since early this morning. _____ already _____ twenty patients, and it's only two o'clock. _____ the other patients in her waiting room yet.

3. Dave likes to swim. _____ for an hour and a half. _____ already _____ across the pool thirty times.

4. Amy is very tired. _____ to job interviews for the past three weeks. _____ already _____ to ten job interviews, and she hasn't found a job yet!

5. Gregory loves to talk. _____ all evening. _____ already _____ about his job, his house, and his car. Fortunately, _____ about his cats yet.

6. Betty and Bob are writing thank-you notes for their wedding gifts, and they're very tired. _____ them all weekend. _____ already _____ to their aunts, uncles, and cousins, but _____ to their friends yet.

7. Andrew is tired. He's having a party tonight, and _____ _____ desserts since early this morning. _____ already _____ two apple pies and three blueberry pies. But he isn't finished. _____ a chocolate cake yet.

8. Patty is very tired. _____ since she got home from school. _____ already _____ English and math. And she'll be up late tonight because _____ for her history test yet.

9. Today is Howard's day off, and he's enjoying himself. _____ _____ since early this morning. _____ already _____ three short stories. But _____ today's newspaper yet.

10. Mr. and Mrs. Grumble like to complain. _____ all evening. _____ already _____ about their jobs, the weather, and several members of their family. Fortunately, they _____ about the party yet, but I'm sure they will.

L LISTENING

Listen and decide where the conversation is taking place.

1. (a.) in a kitchen
   b. in a supermarket

2. a. at home
   b. in school

3. a. in a department store
   b. in a laundromat

4. a. at a movie theater
   b. at home

5. a. at a clinic
   b. at a bakery

6. a. in a cafeteria
   b. in a library

7. a. at a concert hall
   b. at a museum

8. a. at a health club
   b. in a book store

9. a. in an office
   b. at a bus stop

10. a. at a zoo
    b. in a pet shop

11. a. at home
    b. at a movie theater

12. a. at a clinic
    b. in a department store

M WHICH WORD?

1. The floor is wet! How long has the ceiling been **(leaking)** / leaked ?

2. I'm not nervous. I've been flown / **flying** in helicopters for years.

3. I'm a little worried. I've never been running / **run** in a marathon before.

4. How many pizzas have you already **made** / been making so far today?

5. You look tired. What have you / **have you been** doing today?

6. I think I've **seen** / been seeing this movie before.

7. Has your husband already giving / **given** blood?

8. I've never **taken** / been taking a karate lesson. Have you?

9. Have you ever been going / **gone** out on a date before?

10. Alexander, your cell phone has rung / **has been ringing** since we started class!

11. Jane isn't nervous. She's been sung / **singing** in front of audiences for years.

YOU DECIDE: *What Are They Saying?*

A. Mrs. Vickers, could I speak to you for a few minutes?

B. Of course. Please sit down.

A. Mrs. Vickers, I've been thinking. I've been working here at the

_____ Company (for/since) _____ .
I've worked very hard, and I've done a lot of things here.

For example, I've _____ ,

I've _____ ,

and I've been _____

(for/since) _____ .

B. That's true, Mr. Mills. And we're happy with your work.

A. Thank you, Mrs. Vickers. As I was saying, I know I've done a
very good job here, and I really think I should get a raise.

I haven't had a raise (for/since) _____ .

B. _____ .

A. _____ .

A. Dad, could I speak to you for a few minutes?

B. Sure, James. Please sit down.

A. Dad, I've been thinking. I've been working very hard in school
this year, and I've done all my chores at home. For example,

I've _____ , I've _____

_____ , and I've been _____

_____ (for/since) _____ .

B. That's true, James. Your mother and I are very proud of you.

A. Thank you, Dad. As I was saying, I know I've been very
responsible, and I really think I should be able to take your
car when I go out on a date. After all, I've been driving

(for/since) _____ .

B. _____ .

A. _____ .

Daniel has been living in a small town in Mexico all his life. His father just got a good job in the United States, and Daniel and his family are going to live there. Daniel's life is going to be very different in the United States.

1. He's going to live in a big city.
2. He's going to take English lessons.
3. He's going to take the subway.
4. He's going to shop in American supermarkets.
5. He's going to eat American food.
6. He's going to play American football.

7. He's going to _____ .

Daniel is a little nervous.

1. _____He's never lived in a big city_____ before.

2. _____ before.

3. _____ before.

4. _____ before.

5. _____ before.

6. _____ before.

7. _____ before.

Daniel's cousins have been living in the United States for many years. They'll be able to help him.

8. _____They've been living in a big city_____ for years.

9. _____ for years.

10. _____ for years.

11. _____ for years.

12. _____ for years.

13. _____ for years.

14. _____ for years.

Daniel's cousins tell him he shouldn't worry. They're sure he'll enjoy his new life in the United States very much.

YOU DECIDE: *A New Life*

_____ has been living in _____

all her life. Now she's going to move to _____ .
                                              (your city)

Her life is going to be very different in _____ .
                                         (your city)

1. She's going to _____ .
2. She's going to _____ .
3. She's going to _____ .
4. She's going to _____ .
5. She's going to _____ .

_____ is a little nervous.

6. _____ before.
7. _____ before.
8. _____ before.
9. _____ before.
10. _____ before.

_____ (has/have) been living in _____ for many
years and will be able to help her.

11. _____ for years.
12. _____ for years.
13. _____ for years.
14. _____ for years.
15. _____ for years.

_____ shouldn't worry. I'm sure she'll enjoy her new life in _____
very much.

Activity Workbook   **75**

A. Complete the sentences with the present perfect.

Ex. (do)   Julie __has__ already __done__ her homework.

   (read)   I __haven't read__ your report yet.

(eat)   **1.** Mary and her brother _____ already _____ breakfast.

(take)   **2.** My nephew _____ his violin lesson yet.

(write)   **3.** I _____ to my grandparents yet.

(go)   **4.** My wife _____ already _____ to work.

(pay)   **5.** You _____ your electric bill yet.

(have)   **6.** Henry _____ already _____ a problem with his new cell phone.

B. Complete the questions.

1. A. _____ to your supervisor yet?

   B. Yes, I have. I spoke to her this morning.

2. A. _____ his new bicycle yet?

   B. Yes, he has. He rode it this morning.

3. A. _____ their paychecks yet?

   B. Yes, they have. They got them this afternoon.

4. A. _____ ever _____ in a helicopter?

   B. Yes, he has. He flew in a helicopter last summer.

5. A. _____ ever _____ on TV?

   B. Yes, she has. She was on TV last week.

6. A. _____ your daughter's new boyfriend yet?

   B. No, I haven't. I'm going to meet him tonight.

C. Complete the sentences.

Ex. My neck is very stiff. _____It's been_____ stiff since I got up this morning.

   Tom is reading his e-mail. ___He's been reading___ it for a half hour.

1. It's sunny. _____ all week.

2. We're browsing the web. _____ the web since 8 o'clock.

3. My daughter has a fever. _____ a fever since early this morning.

4. My son is studying. _____ since he got home from school.

5. Our neighbors are arguing. _____ all afternoon.

6. I know how to skate. _____ how to skate since I was six years old.

7. Susan is interested in science. _____ interested in science since she was a teenager.

8. My husband and I are cleaning our basement. _____ it all weekend.

D. Complete the answers.

| for | since |

1. How long has your wife been working at the bank?

_____ 1999.

2. How long have those dogs been barking?

_____ a long time.

3. How long has it been snowing?

_____ two days.

4. How long have you wanted to be an astronaut?

_____ I was six years old.

E. Complete the sentences.

1. My brother owns a motorcycle. _____ a motorcycle since last summer.

Before that, _____ a bicycle.

2. I'm a journalist. _____ a journalist since 2000.

Before that, _____ an actor.

3. My daughter likes classical music. _____ classical music since she finished college.

Before that, _____ rock music.

F. Listen and choose the correct answer.

1. a. Janet is in acting school.
   b. Janet is an actress.

2. a. The president has finished his speech.
   b. The president is still speaking.

3. a. They've been living in New York since 1995.
   b. They haven't lived in New York since 1995.

4. a. They're going to eat later.
   b. They're going to eat now.

5. a. She's called the superintendent.
   b. She has to call the superintendent.

6. a. Someone is helping Billy with his homework.
   b. No one is helping Billy with his homework.

| enjoy _____ing | like to _____ | _____ing |

1. My wife and I ____enjoy____ relaxing on the beach when we go on vacation.

2. Mrs. Finn is very talkative. She _____likes to_____ talk about her grandchildren.

   ____Talking____ about her grandchildren is important to her.

3. Billy doesn't _____ going to the doctor, but he went yesterday for his annual checkup.

4. I _____ knit sweaters. _____ sweaters is a good way to relax.

5. My husband doesn't _____ asking for a raise, but sometimes he has to.

6. Dr. Brown _____ deliver babies. In her opinion, _____ babies is the best job in the world.

7. Bob doesn't _____ being a bachelor. He thinks _____ married is better.

8. Ann _____ plant flowers. She thinks _____ flowers is good exercise.

9. Jim _____ chatting online with his friends, but his parents think _____ online every evening isn't a very good idea.

10. Tom doesn't _____ play hockey. He thinks _____ hockey is dangerous.

11. My parents go to the gym during the winter, but in the summer they _____ going hiking.

12. Martin _____ go to parties. He thinks _____ to parties is a good way to meet people.

13. I really want to play the piano well, but I don't _____ practicing.

Listen. Then clap and practice.

Writing is   fun.

I like to   write.

I enjoy   writing letters   late   at night.

Eating is   fun.

I like to   eat.

I enjoy eating   fish,   and I like eating   meat.

Skiing is   great.

He likes to   ski.

But skiing's been   hard   since he hurt   his knee.

Singing is   fun.

She likes to   sing.

But today   she's sick,   and she can't sing   a thing.

Running is   great.

They like to   run.

Swimming's   okay,   but running's   more fun.

Baking is   great.

He likes to   bake.

When he's feeling   sad,   he bakes   a cake.

Knitting is   fun.

She likes to   knit.

She enjoys knitting   sweaters,   but none of them   fit!

clean	complain	eat	go	sit	wear
cleaning	complaining	eating	going	sitting	wearing

1. I hate to _____complain_____, but your loud music is disturbing me.

2. Carol tries to avoid _____ in the sun.

3. Sally likes to _____ dinner at home.

4. My son hates to _____ his room.

5. Richard can't stand to _____ a tie.

6. Tom avoids _____ his apartment whenever he can.

7. James doesn't like to _____ to the mall.

8. My husband and I hate _____ sailing.

9. My wife and I like to _____ in the park on a sunny day.

10. Please try to avoid _____ about the weather all the time.

11. My friends and I can't stand _____ in fast-food restaurants.

12. My daughter likes _____ the sweater you gave her for her birthday.

D   **GRAMMARRAP: Pet Peeves**

Listen. Then clap and practice.

I don't like	waiting	for the bus	in the rain.
I hate to	rush	when I'm late	for a plane.
I avoid	talking	to strangers	on the train.
I can't stand	driving	in the center	lane.

I don't like to	iron	on a hot	summer day.
I hate to clean	the house	in the middle	of May.
I avoid	dusting	and sweeping	my floors.
I can't stand	doing	all my household	chores!

1. David is happy he works in a gym because he enjoys

   exercising every day .

2. Gloria hates being a taxi driver because she can't stand

   .

3. Miguel is glad he lives in Puerto Rico because he likes

   .

4. I'm sorry I'm a secretary because I can't stand

   .

5. We're happy we're going camping because we enjoy

   .

6. William is upset he's sick because he hates

   .

7. I'm glad I have a new bicycle because I like

   .

8. Norman doesn't like being on a diet because he can't stand

   .

9. Julie is happy she's a Hollywood actress because she enjoys

   .

MY ENERGETIC GRANDFATHER

A. Your grandfather is very energetic!

B. He sure is!

A. When did he start _____ [1] the drums?

B. Believe it or not, he learned _____ [2] the drums when he was sixty years old!

A. That's incredible! Does he _____ [3] the drums often?

B. Yes, he does. He's played every day for the last eight years.

A. What else does he enjoy doing?

B. He enjoys _____ [4], he enjoys _____ [5], and he also enjoys _____ [6].

A. I hope I have that much energy when I'm his age!

G **I CAN'T STAND IT!**

> I spoke with my friend Pam last weekend, and she talked a lot about figure skating. Ever since she started to figure skate several months ago, that's all she ever talks about! I never go out with her anymore because she practices figure skating all the time. And whenever I talk to her on the phone, figure skating is the only thing she talks about! (She thinks that everybody should learn to figure skate.) I can't stand it! I don't ever want to hear another word about figure skating!

Now YOU tell about somebody.

I spoke to my friend _____ last weekend, and _____ talked a lot about

_____. Ever since _____

_____

_____

_____

_____

_____

CHOOSE

1. I've decided | buy / buying / (to buy) | a motorcycle.

2. Have you ever considered | to move / moving / move | ?

3. I'm thinking about | going / to go / go | on a diet.

4. You should consider | to change / change / changing | jobs.

5. Have you decided to | get / to get / getting | a dog?

6. He's thought about | to retire / retiring / retire | .

I **GRAMMARRAP:** *I Considered Ordering the Cheesecake*

Listen. Then clap and practice.

I considered   ordering the cheesecake.
Everyone   said I should   try it.
But then   I decided   to skip   dessert.
I wanted to   stay   on my diet.

I thought about   going   home early.
It was only   a quarter to   ten.
But I changed   my mind and   decided to   stay
When the music   started   again.

I thought about   moving to   France
And studying   music and   dance.
But I changed   my mind and   decided to   stay
With my cat   and my bird and my   plants.

A. Hi, Carla. How are you? We haven't spoken in a long time. Tell me, what have you been doing?

B. ....

A. Oh. And what are you thinking about doing after you finish studying English?

B. For a while, I considered .... ,

and then I thought about ....

But I finally decided to ....

A. Oh. Why did you decide to do that?

B. Because ....

A. That's interesting. Tell me, Carla, have you ever considered ....

.... ?

B. Yes. I thought about doing that, but decided it wasn't a very good idea.

A. Why not?

B. Because ....

A. Oh, I see.

B. So, Kathy, do you think I'm making the right decision?

A. ....

B. Do you really think so?

A. ....

B. Well, it was great talking to you. Let's get together soon.

A. Okay. I'll call you and we'll make some plans.

WHAT'S THE WORD?

1. You can't keep on _____rearranging_____ the furniture so often. You rearranged it last weekend!

2. I stopped ___eiting___ meat. I only eat fish and chicken.

3. He tried to quit ___worring___, but he couldn't. He still worries about everything.

4. Alice always gets up late. She should start ___getting___ up earlier.

5. Richard doesn't exercise very often. He should begin ___exersising___ every day. He'll feel a lot better.

6. You can't continue ___asking___ me the same question. You've already asked me ten times!

7. I realize that I can't keep on ___arguing___ with people. I'm never going to argue with anyone again!

8. I know that Dave takes piano lessons. When did he start ___taking___ guitar lessons?

9. You should stop ___paing___ your bills late and start ___paing___ them on time.

10. Professor Blaine is very boring. Students continue ___falling___ asleep in his classes.

L **GOOD DECISIONS**

bite	clean	cook	do	gossip	interrupt	make	pay

This year I'm going to break all my bad habits. First, I've decided to stop ___biting___ [1] my nails. I've also started _____ [2] exercises every day. I learned _____ [3] when I was young, so I've decided to start _____ [4] healthy meals. I'm also considering _____ [5] my bills on time, and I'm thinking about _____ [6] my apartment every week. I've also decided to stop _____ [7] about other people and to stop _____ [8] my friends while they're talking.

1.
My husband can't stop ____falling____ asleep at the movies. Every time we go, he falls asleep. If he keeps on _____ asleep, I'll never go to a movie with him again.

2.
I don't think I should continue _____ weights every day. I like _____ weights, but I'm afraid I might hurt my back if I keep on _____ them so often.

3.
My older sister always teases me. Today I'm really mad! She began _____ me early this morning, and she hasn't stopped. If she keeps on _____ me, I'm going to cry. And I won't stop _____ until she stops _____ me!

4.
My friend Albert has got to stop _____ so fast and start _____ more carefully. If he continues _____ fast, I'm sure he'll have a serious accident some day.

5.
Mr. Perkins, when are you going to stop _____ so sloppily and start _____ more neatly? If you keep on _____ like that, I'm going to have to fire you.

6.
My boyfriend is very clumsy. When we go dancing, he keeps on _____ on my feet. If he doesn't start _____ more gracefully, I'm going to stop _____ dancing with him.

LISTENING

Listen and choose the correct answer.

1. a. delivering babies.
   b. fix broken legs.

2. a. eating junk food.
   b. to pay our bills late.

3. a. swimming.
   b. to play golf.

4. a. to tap dance.
   b. figure skating.

5. a. to work out at a health club every week.
   b. retiring.

6. a. taking karate lessons.
   b. mend my pants.

7. a. to go back to college?
   b. moving?

8. a. to argue with people.
   b. biting my nails.

9. a. teasing your sister?
   b. to go to bed so late?

10. a. eat fruits and vegetables.
    b. worrying about my health all the time.

11. a. stand in line.
    b. wearing a suit.

12. a. taking photographs?
    b. study the piano?

13. a. to assemble his VCR.
    b. clean his apartment.

14. a. studying engineering.
    b. teach a computer course.

15. a. to live at home.
    b. going to school for the rest of your life.

O **WHAT DOES IT MEAN?**

Choose the correct answer.

1. My wife is very dizzy.
   a. I'm glad to hear that.
   b. How long has she been feeling sick?
   c. I guess she has a lot of things to do.

2. Peter and Nancy are vegetarians.
   a. They've quit eating vegetables.
   b. They've stopped planting flowers.
   c. They've stopped eating meat.

3. Andrew avoids talking about politics.
   a. He doesn't like talking about politics.
   b. He enjoys talking about politics.
   c. He's learning to talk about politics.

4. Shirley has worked her way to the top.
   a. She's the tallest person in her family.
   b. She's the president of her company.
   c. She works on the top floor of her building.

5. The people across the street were furious.
   a. They were embarrassed.
   b. They were awkward.
   c. They were very angry.

6. What's your present occupation?
   a. What do you do now?
   b. What are you going to do?
   c. What did you do when you were young?

7. This is my father-in-law, Mr. Kramer.
   a. He just graduated from high school.
   b. He just retired.
   c. He's seventeen years old.

8. My mother is going to mend my socks.
   a. She's going to fix them.
   b. She's going to wash them.
   c. She's going to send them to my sister.

9. You should stop gossiping.
   a. You should stop interrupting people.
   b. You should stop bumping into people.
   c. You should stop talking about people.

10. I've decided to ask for a raise.
    a. You should speak to your landlord.
    b. You should speak to your boss.
    c. You should speak to your instructor.

11. Dr. Wu has a lot of patients.
    a. That's true. She never gets angry.
    b. I know. She's a very popular doctor.
    c. That's true. She never gets sick.

12. My Uncle Gino has an Italian accent.
    a. He bought it when he went to Italy.
    b. He wears it all the time.
    c. Everybody knows he's from Italy.

1. Lisa didn't feel very well when she got up this morning because

   she *(eat)* ___had___ ___eaten___ a lot of candy before she went to bed.

2. My husband invited his boss for dinner last Friday night, and he forgot to tell me.

   Unfortunately, I *(get)* _____ already _____ tickets for a concert.

3. Our friends didn't stop showing us pictures of their grandson all evening. They

   (visit) _____ just _____ him the day before.

4. I wanted to drive to the mountains with my friends yesterday, but they *(drive)* _____

   _____ to the mountains the afternoon before.

5. Andrew wasn't very happy when I visited him yesterday. He *(cut)* _____ just _____
   himself while he was cooking dinner.

6. Alice couldn't buy the new printer she wanted because she *(spend)* _____ _____
   all her money on her vacation.

7. When my son got home from his date last night, my wife and I *(go)* _____ already

   _____ to sleep.

8. My children didn't want to eat pancakes for breakfast yesterday morning because

   I *(make)* _____ _____ pancakes the morning before.

9. I didn't see a movie with my friends last weekend because I *(see)* _____ _____
   three movies the weekend before.

10. When I got up this morning, my wife *(leave)* _____ already _____ for work.

11. Norman was upset when I saw him yesterday morning. He *(have)* _____ _____
    a big argument with his next-door neighbor the night before.

12. When I saw Jill today, she was very happy. Her boyfriend *(give)* _____ just _____
    her a beautiful bracelet for her birthday.

13. Tom couldn't lend me his dictionary the other day because he *(lose)* _____ _____
    it the week before.

Listen. Then clap and practice.

She felt very   happy   when she left   the store.
She had never   bought   a computer   before.

He looked   very nervous when he knocked   on the door.
He had never   gone out   on a date   before.

She felt very   weak,   and her throat was   sore.
She had never   had   the flu   before.

He felt   very proud   when his guests asked for   more.
He had never   baked   a pie   before.

She felt   very foolish   when her food   hit the floor.
She had never   eaten   with chopsticks   before.

He looked   very scared   when it started to   roar.
He had never   been close   to a lion   before.

She was very   annoyed   when he started to   snore.
He had never   made   so much noise   before.

He was very   surprised   when he opened   the drawer.
He had never   seen   so much money   before.

C. LATE FOR EVERYTHING

Gary Gray was very upset yesterday. He didn't get up until 9:00, and as a result, he was late for everything all day!

Today's meeting begins at 10:00.

2. He drove to the office and arrived late for an important meeting.

It _____ already _____.

Bank Closes at 3:00.

4. He got to the bank at 3:15, but he was too late. It _____ already _____.

To: garyg@go.com
From: tom@hopmail.com

I'll be leaving at 4:30. Hope to see you before then.

6. He had made plans to get together with his friend Tom. But he didn't get to Tom's office until 5:00. His friend Tom

_____ already _____.

Last train to Centerville leaves at 9:30.

1. He got to the train station at 9:45. The train ___had___ already ____left____.

To: garyg@go.com
From: janet@hopmail.com

Let's have lunch at 12:00. I have to go back to work at 12:45.

3. He got to the restaurant at 1:00 to meet his friend Janet for lunch. However, she

_____ already _____ back to work.

Professor Tweedle's Lecture on Bird-Watching Starts at 4:00.

5. He got to the bird-watching lecture at

4:15. It _____ already _____.

Dear Gary,
    Our plane will be arriving at the airport at 8:10. We're looking forward to seeing you.
        Love,
        Grandma & Grandpa

7. He drove to the airport to pick up his grandmother and grandfather. He got to the airport at 8:30. Their plane

_____ already _____.

1. We got lost on the way to the party last night. We *(listen)* ___hadn't___ ___listened___ very carefully to the directions.

2. I enjoyed seeing my old friends at my high school reunion last weekend.

   I *(see)* _____ _____ them since we finished high school.

3. My wife and I decided to have a picnic in the park last Sunday. We *(have)* _____

   _____ a picnic in the park in a long time.

4. I went dancing with my girlfriend last Saturday night, and I hurt my back.

   I *(go)* _____ _____ dancing in a long time.

5. Cynthia was embarrassed at her party last night. She had invited her cousin Charles, but

   she *(remember)* _____ _____ to invite his girlfriend, Louise.

6. Frank looked terrible when I saw him yesterday. His pants were dirty, he

   (iron) _____ _____ his shirt, and he *(shave)* _____ _____
   in several days.

7. Michael was very discouraged when I saw him last week. He had been on a diet for a month,

   and he *(lose)* _____ _____ any weight.

8. Sylvia fell several times while she was skiing last weekend. She *(ski)* _____

   _____ in a long time.

9. Arnold's boss fired him last week. Arnold *(get)* _____ _____ to work on time
   in six months.

10. Betty was very lucky she didn't miss her plane this morning. She got to the airport late, but

    the plane *(take off)* _____ _____ yet.

11. Alan did poorly on his English exam last week. I'm not surprised. He *(study)* _____

    _____ for the test.

12. Stuart enjoyed riding his bicycle last weekend. He *(ride)* _____ _____ it in a
    long time.

WORKING HARD

Jennifer was very busy after school yesterday.

1:00	write an English composition
2:00	study for my science test
3:00	practice the trombone
4:00	read the next history chapter
5:00	memorize my lines for the school play

What was she doing at 2:00?

1. _____ She was studying for her science test. _____

What had she already done?

2. _____ She had already written an English composition. _____

What hadn't she done yet?

3. _____ She hadn't practiced the trombone yet. _____

4. _____

5. _____

Brian had a very busy day at the office yesterday.

9:00	send an e-mail to the boss
10:00	give the employees their paychecks
11:00	hook up the new printer
1:00	write to the Bentley Company
2:00	take two packages to the post office

What was he doing at 11:00?

6. _____

What had he already done?

7. _____

8. _____

What hadn't he done yet?

9. _____

10. _____

Mr. and Mrs. Mendoza had a very busy day
at home yesterday.

8:00	assemble Billy's new bicycle
9:00	fix the fence
11:00	clean the garage
2:00	repair the roof
4:00	start to build a tree house

What were they doing at 11:00?

11. _____

What had they already done?

12. _____

13. _____

What hadn't they done yet?

14. _____

15. _____

Brenda wants to lose some weight, so she had
a very busy day at her health club.

9:00	do yoga
10:00	go jogging
12:00	play squash
3:00	lift weights
4:00	swim across the pool 10 times

What was she doing at 12:00?

16. _____

What had she already done?

17. _____

18. _____

What hadn't she done yet?

19. _____

20. _____

F WHAT HAD THEY BEEN DOING?

1. Professor Smith finally ended his lecture at 6:00. He *(talk)* _____had been talking_____ for three hours.

2. The Millers moved out of their apartment building last week. They *(live)* _____ _____ there for several years.

3. Our daughter lost her job last week. She *(work)* _____ at the same company since she graduated from college.

4. Peter was happy when he and his girlfriend finally got married. They *(go out)* _____ _____ for eight years.

5. We were sad when Rudy's Restaurant closed. We *(plan)* _____ to eat there on our anniversary.

6. We felt very nostalgic when we went back to our hometown. We *(think about)* _____ _____ going back there for a long time.

7. My husband and I were happy when our son decided to study harder. He *(get)* _____ _____ poor grades in school.

8. Mr. Best was happy when his neighbor bought his own ladder. He *(borrow)* _____ _____ Mr. Best's ladder for many years.

9. I'm not surprised that Lenny's doctor put him on a diet. Lenny *(eat)* _____ too many fatty foods.

10. It's too bad your daughter wasn't able to perform in her violin recital last weekend. She *(rehearse)* _____ for it for a long time.

11. I'm sorry you had to cancel your trip to Hawaii. You and your wife *(look forward)* _____ _____ to it for a long time.

12. I'm so happy that Sally won the marathon last weekend. She *(train)* _____ for it for the past six months.

13. Nobody at the office was surprised when Mrs. Anderson fired Frank, her new assistant. He *(arrive)* _____ late for work every day for the past month.

GRAMMARRAP: *George Had Been Thinking of Studying Greek*

Listen. Then clap and practice.

George had been　thinking of　　studying　　Greek,

Moving to　　　　Athens　and learning　to speak.

But he changed　　his mind　　and decided to　　stay

With his family　　and friends　and his dog　　in L.A.

Jill had been　　planning to　　learn how to　　ski,

But she tripped and　　fell and　　sprained　her knee.

She had been　dreaming of　mountains and　snow.

But now she's　at home and has　no place　to go.

Marie had been　planning to　marry　　Tim,

But she fell　　in love　with his brother,　Jim.

Jim had been　thinking of　marrying　Dee,

But everything　changed when he met　Marie.

H **LISTENING**

Listen to each word and then say it.

1. retire

2. memorize

3. practice

4. drug store

5. favorite

6. interrupt

7. around

8. restaurant

9. lively

10. loudly

11. swollen

12. elevator

13. fly

14. believe

15. cold

16. fall asleep

1 MARYLOU'S BROKEN KEYBOARD

Marylou's keyboard is broken. The r's and the l's don't always work. Fill in the missing r's and l's, and then read Marylou's letters aloud.

1.

_R_ oger,

I'm af _r_ aid the__e's something w__ong with the fi__ep__ace in the __iving __oom. A__so, the __ef__ige__ato__ is b__oken. I've been ca____ing the __and__o__d fo__ th__ee days on his ce____ phone, but he hasn't ca____ed back. I hope he ca____s me tomo____ow.

Ma__y__ou

2.

__ouise,

I'm te____ib__y wo____ied about my b__othe__ La____y's hea__th. He hu__t his __eg whi__e he was p__aying baseba____. He had a____eady dis__ocated his shou__der whi__e he was su__fing __ast F__iday. Acco__ding to his docto__, he is a__so having p__ob__ems with his b__ood p__essu__e and with his __ight w__ist. He __ea____y should t__y to __e__ax and take __ife a __itt__e easie__.

Ma__y__ou

3.

A__no__d,

Can you possib__y __ecommend a good __estau__ant in you__ neighbo__hood? I'm p__anning on taking my re__atives to __unch tomo____ow, but I'm not su__e whe__e.

We ate at a ve__y nice G__eek __estau__ant nea__ you__ apa__tment bui__ding __ast month, but I haven't been ab__e to __emembe__ the name. Do you know the p__ace?

You__ f__iend,
Ma__y__ou

4.

__osa,

I have been p__anning a t__ip to F__o__ida. I'____ be f__ying to O____ando on F__iday, and I'____ be __etu__ning th__ee days __ater. Have you eve__ been the__e? I __emembe__ you had fami__y membe__s who __ived in F__o__ida seve__a__ yea__s ago.

P__ease w__ite back.

A____ my __ove,
Ma__y__ou

Listen and choose the correct answer.

1. a. He can't find it anywhere.
   b. Where can it be?
   c. Nobody can hear him.

2. a. No, she isn't. She's my wife.
   b. Yes. She's my wife's cousin.
   c. No. She works for a different company.

3. a. Did you take a lot of photographs?
   b. Why did you charge it?
   c. That's too bad. You had been looking forward to it.

4. a. I know. He missed all his tests.
   b. I know. He's been doing very poorly.
   c. I know. He hasn't had a bad grade yet.

5. a. Did she find it?
   b. Whose is it?
   c. I'm sure it hurt a lot.

6. a. We stayed for the lecture.
   b. We talked about classical music.
   c. We read about psychology.

7. a. Did you enjoy yourselves?
   b. How many miles did you travel?
   c. Where did you drive?

8. a. She's having problems with her feet.
   b. She's having problems with her teeth.
   c. That's okay. We all make mistakes.

9. a. Did he make it?
   b. When did you get home?
   c. I know. He likes everything you serve.

10. a. You're right. I bought one.
    b. No, but I heard the noise.
    c. Sorry. We don't sell motorcycles.

11. a. I think so. He's been working hard.
    b. Yes. His plane will leave soon.
    c. I hope so. He never goes to work.

12. a. Poor Amy! She's always sick.
    b. Amy needs a new pair of boots.
    c. She was afraid to ask for it.

13. a. What a shame! Now she can't sing.
    b. What a shame! Now she can't knit.
    c. What a shame! Now she can't walk.

14. a. Would you like to talk about it?
    b. Who are you going to give it to?
    c. What did you decide to do?

15. a. I like you, too.
    b. What are you going to send me?
    c. You don't have anything to be jealous about.

16. a. Was it a very bad accident?
    b. Do you know anybody who can fix it?
    c. How long had they been going out?

17. a. I hope he feels better soon.
    b. What happened? Did you twist it?
    c. How are your cousins?

18. a. Did you call the doctor?
    b. What had you eaten?
    c. Why were you sad?

19. a. I'm glad to hear that.
    b. What was he angry about?
    c. What did he ask them?

20. a. We enjoyed the music.
    b. The lecture was very boring.
    c. The food was excellent.

21. a. They're too small.
    b. You have a job interview today.
    c. You have a baseball game today.

22. a. She enjoys going to the symphony.
    b. She enjoys going window-shopping.
    c. She enjoys doing gymnastics.

23. a. We're going to have a party.
    b. We're going on vacation.
    c. We received a lot of anniversary gifts.

24. a. He's glad he bought it.
    b. He's going to wear it for several years.
    c. He has to return it on Tuesday.

✓ CHECK-UP TEST: Chapters 7–8

A. Complete the sentences with the appropriate verb form.

(eat) 1. Why do you keep on _____ junk food?

(wrestle) 2. My mother thinks _____ is dangerous.

(stop) 3. I've decided _____ interrupting people all the time.

(box) 4. Bruno practices _____ every day at the gym.

(swim) 5. _____ is a good way to relax.

(skate) 6. Where did your daughter learn _____ so well?

(talk) 7. Please stop _____. I'm trying to sleep!

(do) 8. Rita thinks that _____ exercises is a good way to start the day.

B. Complete the sentences, using the past perfect tense.

Ex. *(wear)* I wore my favorite striped tie to work yesterday. I ____hadn't worn____ it to work in a long time.

(start) By the time Andrew got to the play, it ___had___ already ___started___.

(speak) 1. I had dinner with some Japanese friends last night. I enjoyed myself very much

because I _____ Japanese in a long time.

(do) 2. By the time Jennifer's father got home from work, she _____ already

_____ her homework, and she was ready to play baseball in the yard with

him.

(leave) 3. Ronald was upset. By the time he got to the train, it _____ already

_____.

(write) 4. I wrote an e-mail to my grandparents last night because I _____

to them for a few weeks.

(have) 5. Patty had pizza for lunch yesterday. She _____ pizza in a long

time.

(take) 6. My husband and I took a walk after dinner last night. We _____

a walk after dinner in a long time.

(eat) 7. I ate a big piece of chocolate cake last night and felt terrible about it. I _____

_____ a rich dessert since I started my diet.

(go) 8. My parents went back to their hometown last month. They _____

back there for twenty years.

C. Complete the sentences, using the past perfect continuous tense.

Ex. *(study)*   Jonathan was glad he did well on his astronomy exam. He ___had been studying___ for it for days.

(work)   **1.**   Marvin didn't get his promotion at work. He was heartbroken because he

_____ overtime for several months.

(train)   **2.**   I was disappointed they canceled the marathon last week. I _____

_____ for it since last summer.

(argue)   **3.**   Jane and John broke up last night. They _____
with each other for the past several weeks.

(plan)   **4.**   Nancy caught a cold and couldn't go on her camping trip. It's a shame because she

_____ it since last April.

D. Listen and choose the correct answer.

Ex.   ⓐ   go fishing.
    b.   going canoeing.

1.   a.   tease her little brother.
    b.   interrupting people.

2.   a.   moving to Miami.
    b.   to sell our house.

3.   a.   to buy a sports car.
    b.   buying a sports car.

4.   a.   waiting in line.
    b.   drive downtown.

5.   a.   going out with Richard.
    b.   ask for a raise.

A WHAT ARE THEY SAYING?

1. A. Did you pick up Rover at the vet?

   B. No. I didn't ____pick him up____.
   I thought YOU did.

3. A. You should take back these library books.

   B. I know. I'll _____
   tomorrow morning.

5. A. Where should we hang up this portrait?

   B. Let's _____
   over the fireplace.

7. A. Are you ever going to throw out these old souvenirs?

   B. I'll _____
   some day.

9. A. Did your daughter take down the photographs of her old boyfriend?

   B. Yes. She _____
   as soon as they stopped going out.

2. A. Did you turn on the heat?

   B. Yes. I _____ a few
   hours ago, but it's still cold in here.

4. A. Has Diane filled out her income tax forms?

   B. No. She's going to _____
   this weekend.

6. A. I'm having trouble hooking up my computer.

   B. No problem. I'll _____.

8. A. Did Sally take back her cell phone to the store?

   B. Yes. She _____
   this afternoon.

10. A. Did you remember to call up Aunt Clara to wish her "Happy Birthday"?

    B. Sorry. I didn't _____.
    I forgot it was her birthday.

| bring back | hand in | put away | put on | take off | turn off | turn on | wake up |

1. I think we should __turn on__ the air conditioner. It's getting very hot in here.

   Good idea. I'll _____ right away.

2. When are you going to __hand__ your biology report __in__?

   I'm going to _____ tomorrow morning. I have to write it tonight.

3. Let's _____ Mom and Dad! It's 8:00, and they're still sleeping!

   Don't _____. It's Saturday. They don't go to work today.

4. Don't forget to _____ the printer _____ before you leave the office tonight.

   You don't have to worry. I always _____ before I leave.

5. Why don't you _____ your hat and coat? It's warm in here.

   I'll _____ in a few minutes. I'm still a little cold.

6. Susie, when are you going to _____ your toys _____?

   I'm still playing with them. I'll _____ later.

7. Teddy, it's time for bed. _____ your pajamas _____!

   Okay, Dad. I'll _____ in a few minutes.

8. Do you think Richard will _____ his girlfriend _____ to the house after the dance?

   I don't know. Maybe he'll _____. I hope he does. I really want to meet her.

C GRAMMARRAP: *I Don't Know How!*

Listen. Then clap and practice.

A.   Take off your   skis.

        Take them off   now!

B.   I can't take them   off.

        I don't know   how!

A.   Turn off the   engine!

        Turn it off   now!

B.   I can't turn it   off.

        I don't know   how!

A.   Turn on the   oven!

        Turn it on   now!

B.   I can't turn it   on.

        I don't know   how!

A.   Hook up the   printer!

        Hook it up   now!

B.   I can't hook it   up.

        I don't know   how!

A.   Pick up the   suitcase.

        Give it to   Jack.

B.   I can't pick it   up.

        I have   a bad back!

A.   Take back   the videos!

        Take them back today.

B.   I can't take them   back.

      It's a holiday!

cross out	give back	look up	throw away	turn off
do over	hook up	think over	turn down	write down

1. Did your teacher like the composition you wrote about Australian birds?

   No, she didn't. I have to ___do it over___.

2. A. Do we still have the hammer we borrowed from our next-door neighbors?

   B. No, we don't. We _____ a long time ago.

3. A. What's the matter with the answering machine? Is it broken?

   B. No, it isn't. I forgot to _____.

4. A. Are you going to accept the invitation to Roger's wedding?

   B. I don't know. I have to _____ carefully. His wedding is in Alaska.

5. A. What's the weather forecast for tomorrow?

   B. I'm not sure. You should _____ on the Internet.

6. A. Is Kimberly going to the prom with Frank?

   B. No, she isn't. She had to _____ because she already had a date with somebody else.

7. A. What should I do with all these letters from my ex-boyfriend?

   B. I think you should _____.

8. A. What's Walter's new address?

   B. I can't remember. But I know I've _____ somewhere.

9. A. Should I erase all these mistakes in my math homework?

   B. No, I think you should just _____.

10. Why aren't you watching the president's speech on TV?

    I watched it for a while, but it was boring. So I

    _____.

James just moved into a new apartment. What does he have to do?

1. He has to (put away) / throw away his books and his clothes.

2. He has to fill out / hook up his printer and his computer.

3. He has to take out / take back the moving truck he rented.

Jennifer is very happy and excited. She just got engaged. What's she going to do?

4. She's going to wake up / drop off her parents and tell them the news.

5. She's going to call off / call up all her friends.

6. She's going to look up / write down all the things her boyfriend said.

Mr. and Mrs. Baker's aunt and uncle are going to visit them next week. What do the Bakers have to do before then?

7. They have to clean up / take out their apartment.

8. They have to pick out / put away their children's toys.

9. They have to throw out / hook up all their old newspapers.

10. They have to call up / hang up their aunt and uncle's portrait.

| figure out | look up | throw out | use up |
| give back | think over | turn off | wake up |

1. Abigail, will you marry me?

That's a big decision, Howard.

I have to _____think it over_____.

2. A. I've been using my neighbor's screwdriver all summer.

   B. Don't you think it's time to _____?

3. A. Is there any more sugar?

   B. No. We _____. We have to buy some tomorrow.

4. A. I don't know the definition of this word.

   B. You really should _____ in the dictionary.

5. A. This math problem is very difficult.

   B. Maybe your mother can help you _____.

6. A. It's 7:30, and the children are still sleeping.

   B. They're going to be late for school. I'll _____.

7. A. It's really cold in here! Is the air conditioner on?

   B. Yes, it is. I'll _____ right away.

8. A. I'm very embarrassed. These are the worst photographs anyone has ever taken of me.

   B. Well, if they bother you that much, why don't you _____?

G **LISTENING**

Listen and choose the correct answer.

1. a. picked it up.
   b. used it up.

2. a. turn it down.
   b. turn it on.

3. a. take them down.
   b. turn them down.

4. a. think them over.
   b. drop them off.

5. a. hook it up.
   b. look it up.

6. a. give it back?
   b. hand it in?

7. a. throw it out.
   b. figure it out.

8. a. write it down.
   b. use it up.

9. a. pick it up.
   b. clean it up.

call on	get over	look through	pick on	take after
get along with	hear from	look up to	run into	

1. I _____take after_____ my father. We're both athletic, we're both interested in engineering, and we both like to paint. I'm really glad I ___take after him___ .

2. I haven't _____ my son in three weeks. He's at college, and I usually _____ every week!

3. I'm so embarrassed. My teacher _____ me twice in class today, but I didn't know ANY of the answers. I have to study tonight. She might _____ again tomorrow.

4. My husband and I enjoyed _____ our wedding pictures. We hadn't _____ in years.

5. Jack _____ his cold very quickly. I think he _____ fast because he stayed home and took care of himself.

6. I really _____ my grandmother. She's honest, she's intelligent, and she's very generous. I hope someday when I'm a grandmother, my grandchildren will _____, too.

7. I was very surprised. I _____ my old girlfriend at the bank yesterday morning. And then I _____ again at a movie last night.

8. I don't _____ my mother-in-law. We often disagree. All the people in our family _____. Why can't I?

9. Bobby is mean. He _____ his cats all the time. The cats don't like it when Bobby _____.

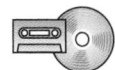

I GRAMMARRAP: *I Don't Get Along with Kate and Clem*

Listen. Then clap and practice.

I don't get along with Kate and Clem.
I almost never hear from them.
But I get along well with Bob and Fay.
I call them up three times a day.

Jack takes after his Uncle Jim.
Bob looks up to his father, Tim.
Kate never picks on her sister, Sue.
But she always picks on her brother, Lou.

J CHOOSE

1. A. Do we have any more pens?
   B. No, we don't. We _____.
      a. ran into them
      b. ran out of them

2. A. Does Carol still have the flu?
   B. No. She _____ a few days ago.
      a. got over it
      b. got it over

3. A. Does Jill get along with her brother?
   B. No. He _____ all the time.
      a. picks her on
      b. picks on her

4. A. I can't remember Tom's phone number.
   B. You should _____.
      a. look up to him
      b. look it up

5. A. Amy knows all the answers in class.
   B. Does the teacher always _____?
      a. call on her
      b. call her on

6. A. This is a very difficult problem.
   B. I know. I can't _____.
      a. figure out it
      b. figure it out

7. A. Have you heard from Pam recently?
   B. Yes. I _____ the other day.
      a. heard her from
      b. heard from her

8. A. What should I do with these old letters?
   B. Why don't you _____?
      a. throw them out
      b. throw out them

9. A. These photographs are wonderful!
   B. I know. Let's _____ again.
      a. look through them
      b. look them through

10. A. Do you like William?
    B. Oh, yes. I _____ very well.
       a. get him along
       b. get along with him

11. A. Should I turn off the computer?
    B. No. You can _____.
       a. leave it on
       b. leave on it

12. A. Did you hang up your uncle's portrait?
    B. No, I didn't. I _____.
       a. took it down
       b. took down it

13. A. You look like your father.
    B. I know. Everybody says I _____.
       a. take him after
       b. take after him

14. A. They have a very unusual last name.
    B. You'll remember it if you _____.
       a. write down it
       b. write it down

K WHAT DOES IT MEAN?

Choose the correct answer.

1. Richard takes after his mother.
   a. He's always with her.
   (b.) They're both shy.
   c. His mother always arrives first.

2. Please turn off the air conditioner.
   a. It's too hot in this room.
   b. The room is too small.
   c. It's too cold in this room.

3. Tom left his briefcase on the plane.
   a. Maybe his mind slipped.
   b. He forgot it.
   c. He was very careful.

4. I'm going to take these pants back.
   a. They're new.
   b. They're medium.
   c. They're too baggy.

5. Fran can't find her notebook.
   a. I hope she didn't throw it out.
   b. I hope she didn't fill it out.
   c. I hope she didn't take it off.

6. Bob doesn't get along with his neighbors.
   a. He can't stand to talk to them.
   b. He likes them very much.
   c. He looks up to them.

7. I hope I don't run into my old boyfriend.
   a. Why? Will he get hurt?
   b. Why don't you want to see him?
   c. Why? Does he like to jog?

8. Paul had to do his homework over.
   a. It was excellent.
   b. He didn't think it over.
   c. He had made a lot of mistakes.

L LISTENING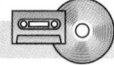

Listen and choose the correct answer.

1. a. He's very tall.
   b. I can never find him.
   (c.) I want to be like him.

2. a. You're lucky he has a car.
   b. I'm sure that bothers you.
   c. Do you also pick him up?

3. a. Yes. I put it in the closet.
   b. Yes. I gave it to our neighbor.
   c. Yes. We had used it all up.

4. a. I'm sorry you're still sick.
   b. I'm glad you're feeling better.
   c. It's too bad you have to do it over.

5. a. No. He speaks very softly.
   b. Yes. He sent me an e-mail yesterday.
   c. No. I haven't heard him recently.

6. a. The music was very loud.
   b. Somebody had picked it up.
   c. I already had another date.

7. a. Yes, several times.
   b. Yes, but I wasn't home.
   c. Yes, but I had already left the house.

8. a. He didn't need it anymore.
   b. It was already at the cleaner's.
   c. I know. He found one he really liked.

9. a. Did she hurt herself?
   b. How did you hurt yourself?
   c. When does her plane leave?

10. a. The store isn't having a sale.
    b. Everything in the store is cheaper.
    c. Everything is 20 cents less this week.

11. a. Good. I'll buy it.
    b. Don't worry. We have larger ones.
    c. I know. It's too tight.

12. a. Yes. I used up four pair.
    b. Yes. I put on four pair.
    c. Yes. I looked up four pair.

1. I ate too much. So _____did I_____.

2. I hate to go to the mall. _____, too.

3. I can play the trombone. So _____.

4. I'm allergic to milk. _____, too.

5. I'll be starting college this fall. _____, too.

6. I was late for work. So _____.

7. I'm going to retire soon. So _____.

8. I've been doing poorly in school recently. _____, too.

9. I just got a promotion. _____, too.

10. I'll be on vacation next week. So _____.

11. I have to lose a little weight. So _____.

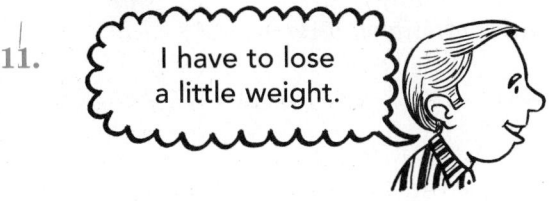

A. Do you live near here?

B. Yes. I live on Center Street.

A. Really? So ___do I___ [1]. I live in the new apartment building at the corner of Center Street and Broadway.

B. What a coincidence! _____ [2], too. I guess we're neighbors. My name is Frank Winters.

A. Hi. I'm Steve Green. Nice to meet you.

B. Nice meeting you, too. So how long have you been living there?

A. I moved in last week.

B. What a coincidence! _____ [3], too. I've been very busy since I got here.

A. So _____ [4]. Moving into a new apartment isn't easy.

B. You're right. It isn't. Tell me, have you found a job yet?

A. Yes, I have. I'll be working at Mason's Department Store.

B. I don't believe it! _____ [5], too.

A. What department will you be working in?

B. I got a job in the Men's Clothing Department.

A. What a coincidence! So _____ [6]. I was a salesperson in my last job also.

B. _____ [7], too. I sold men's clothing.

A. I can't believe it! _____ [8], too.

B. I'm on my way to work right now.

A. _____ [9], too. Do you want to have lunch together?

B. Sure. I have a lunch break at noon.

A. So _____ [10]. Let's meet for lunch in the company cafeteria.

B. Okay. That'll be nice. I'm looking forward to it.

A. So _____ [11].

1. I didn't like the movie.
Neither _____did I_____.

2. I'm not feeling very well.
_____ either.

3. I wasn't in school yesterday.
Neither _____.

4. I can't play tennis very well.
_____ either.

5. I won't be home tonight.
_____ either.

6. I've never been in the hospital before.
Neither _____.

7. I can't stand driving in traffic.
_____ either.

8. I'm not going to order dessert.
Neither _____.

9. I didn't enjoy the lecture.
_____ either.

10. I don't like to practice the piano.
Neither _____.

11. I'll never go sailing again.
Neither _____.

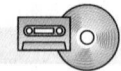
Listen and complete the sentences.

1. So _____*did I*_____ .

2. _____, too.

3. So _____ .

4. _____ either.

5. _____, too.

6. _____, too.

7. Neither _____ .

8. _____, too.

9. Neither _____ .

10. So _____ .

11. _____ either.

12. _____, too.

13. Neither _____ .

14. So _____ .

15. _____ either.

E **GRAMMARRAP:** *So Do I*

Listen. Then clap and practice.

A.   I like to   fly.

B.   So do   I.

A.   They like to   ski.

B.   So do   we.

A.   She likes the   zoo.

B.   He does,   too.

A.   You're a good   friend.

B.   So are   you.

F **GRAMMARRAP:** *They Didn't Either*

Listen. Then clap and practice.

We didn't   eat it.

They didn't   either.

He didn't   finish it.

Neither did   she.

She wasn't   hungry.

He wasn't   either.

They weren't   hungry.

Neither were   we.

1. Why were you and your brother late for school today?

   I had to go to the dentist, and so ___did he___.

2. Will you and your wife be home this evening?

   I don't think so. I'll be working late, and so _____.

3. How did you and Tom feel after you ran in the marathon?

   I was exhausted, and _____, too.

4. Would you and your sister like to learn how to ski?

   Actually, I've already tried it, and so _____.

5. Can Ricky and I go to the movies tonight?

   He should study for his English exam, and _____, too.

6. Have you seen Mr. and Mrs. Martinez recently?

   I saw them today. I was in the park, and _____, too.

7. Should I go into the water with Timmy and Susie?

   No. That's okay. Timmy can swim, and _____ Susie.

8. Why weren't you and your brother at baseball practice today?

   I had to help my mother, and so _____.

9. Why are you and your wife leaving the party?

   She has to get up early tomorrow, and _____, too.

10. Why are your parents so worried?

    I've decided to ...., and _____ my brother.

1. Are you and your brother going to be in the school play?

Unfortunately, he can't act, and neither ___can I___.

2. Why do you and your friends look so upset?

I didn't do very well on the math test, and _____ either.

3. Did you and your son see the baseball game on TV today?

No, we didn't. I'm not interested in sports, and neither _____.

4. Are you and your sister going to go to the concert tonight?

No, we aren't. I don't like folk music, and _____ either.

5. Why did you and your friends leave the dance so early last night?

I wasn't having a very good time, and neither _____.

6. Have you and your wife made plans for your vacation yet?

I haven't had very much time, and _____ either.

7. Are you and your roommates going to Sally's wedding?

No, we aren't. I won't be here this weekend, and neither _____.

8. It's getting late. Should I make dinner now?

The truth is, I'm not very hungry, and the children _____.

9. Is the DVD player still broken?

Yes, it is. I haven't been able to fix it, and _____ your father.

10. How was your date with Samantha last night?

We were both a little nervous. I had never gone out on a date before, and _____ either.

WHAT ARE THEY SAYING?

| so | too | either | neither |

1. A. Why didn't Ronald and his wife go to work yesterday?

   B. He had a terrible cold,

   and { _____ so did she _____ .
         _____ she did, too _____ .

2. A. Did Betty and Bob enjoy the concert last night?

   B. Not really. She couldn't hear the music,

   and { _____ .
         _____ .

3. A. Do Jack and his girlfriend enjoy going sailing?

   B. No, they don't. She gets seasick,

   and { _____ .
         _____ .

4. A. Why didn't Mr. and Mrs. Miller order the cheesecake for dessert?

   B. He doesn't eat rich foods,

   and { _____ .
         _____ .

5. A. Why did Beverly and Brian have trouble doing their chemistry experiments?

   B. He hadn't followed the instructions,

   and { _____ .
         _____ .

6. A. Why aren't you and Peter good friends any more?

   B. I'm in love with Amanda Richardson,

   and { _____ .
         _____ .

1. I'm tall, but my sister and brother _____aren't_____. I've always _____ the tallest person in our family.

2. My brother isn't very athletic, but my sister _____. She enjoys _____ squash and _____ gymnastics.

3. I can't draw pictures, but my brother _____. He's been _____ pictures since he _____ four years old.

4. My brother and I have different interests. I enjoy seeing movies, but my brother _____. He enjoys _____ to lectures and concerts.

5. My mother is interested in photography, but my father _____. My mother _____ photographs since she was a teenager.

6. My father has lived here all his life, but his parents _____. They've _____ in this country _____ fifty years. Before that, they _____ in Italy.

7. My grandparents sometimes speak to us in Italian, but my father _____. He _____ Italian to anyone in a long time.

8. I'll be going to college next year, but my brother _____. He _____ finished high school yet.

9. I don't have a very good voice, but my sister _____. She sings in the school choir. She has _____ in the choir _____ she started high school.

10. I'm usually very neat, but my sister and brother _____. They never hang _____ their clothes or put _____ their books.

11. I know how to ski, but my brother _____. I've been skiing _____ the past nine years.

12. My sister is a very good skater, but my brother and I _____. We just started _____ a month ago. Before that, we _____ never _____ at all.

LISTENING

Listen and complete the sentences.

1. but my husband _____ didn't _____.

2. but my daughter _____.

3. but you _____.

4. but I _____.

5. but my friends _____.

6. but my wife _____.

7. but you _____.

8. but my brother _____.

9. but everybody else _____.

10. but our teacher _____.

11. but my son _____.

12. but the other man _____.

13. but my sister _____.

14. but I _____.

15. but my friends _____.

16. but my brother _____.

17. but my children _____.

18. but I _____.

L **GRAMMARRAP:** *I've Been Working Hard, and You Have, Too*

Listen. Then clap and practice.

I've been working hard, and   you have,   too.

I'm   exhausted,   and so   are you.

He's been   out of town,   and so   has she.

They've been very   busy,   and so   have we.

I   didn't go,   and neither   did he.

They   weren't there,   and neither   were we.

We   stayed home,   and so   did they.

Nobody   went   to the meeting   that day.

I don't speak   Greek,   but my brother   does.

I wasn't born in   Greece,   but my mother   was.

I didn't study   Greek,   but my brother   did.

He's spoken   Greek   since he was   a kid.

Listen to each word and then say it.

f**u**ll		f**oo**l

1.	l**oo**k	3.	p**u**t	1.	n**oo**n	3.	J**u**dy
2.	c**ou**ld	4.	f**oo**t	2.	dr**ew**	4.	f**oo**d

Listen and put a circle around the word that has the same sound.

1.	f**u**ll:	p**oo**l	(c**oo**ks)	sh**oe**
2.	fl**u**:	t**oo**	w**ou**ld	bl**oo**d
3.	g**oo**d:	s**ou**p	sh**ou**ldn't	J**u**ne
4.	w**oo**d:	fl**u**	t**oo**th	p**u**t
5.	c**ou**ld:	c**u**p	c**oo**kies	**u**pstairs
6.	h**oo**k:	f**oo**d	m**o**vie	g**oo**d
7.	w**o**man:	s**u**gar	tr**ue**	n**ew**

Now make a sentence using all the words you circled, and read the sentence aloud.

8. .... much ....
   in their ....

9.	s**ui**t:	tw**o**	p**u**t	b**u**s
10.	c**oo**k:	f**oo**d	b**oo**ks	s**u**nny
11.	f**oo**t:	b**oo**kcase	p**oo**l	m**u**st
12.	bl**ue**:	j**u**st	wh**o**	l**oo**ked
13.	w**ou**ld:	s**ui**t	t**oo**l	t**oo**k
14.	c**oo**l:	st**oo**d	aftern**oo**n	p**u**lse
15.	sch**oo**l:	S**u**san's	th**u**nder	fl**oo**r

Now make a sentence using all the words you circled, and read the sentence aloud.

16. .... from ....
   .... this .... ?

N WHAT DOES IT MEAN?

__j__	1. afford		a.	afraid
_____	2. argue		b.	do poorly
_____	3. bachelor		c.	fight
_____	4. begin		d.	finish
_____	5. bump into		e.	friendly and talkative
_____	6. can't stand		f.	give back
_____	7. compatible		g.	give lessons
_____	8. consider		h.	hate
_____	9. continue		i.	have a lot in common
_____	10. discuss		j.	have enough money
_____	11. exam		k.	how much it costs
_____	12. exhausted		l.	hurt
_____	13. fail		m.	keep on
_____	14. frightened		n.	meet
_____	15. hike		o.	ready
_____	16. injure		p.	recently
_____	17. lately		q.	single man
_____	18. outgoing		r.	someone who doesn't eat meat
_____	19. prepared		s.	start
_____	20. price		t.	study again
_____	21. return		u.	take a long walk
_____	22. review		v.	talk about
_____	23. stand in line		w.	test
_____	24. teach		x.	think about
_____	25. use up		y.	tired
_____	26. vegetarian		z.	wait

✔ **CHECK-UP TEST: Chapters 9-10**

A. Complete the sentences.

Ex. My son is waiting for me at the bus stop. I have to pick ___him___ ___up___ right away.

My mother and I are both tall with curly hair. Everybody says I take ___after___ ___her___.

1. I'll finish my homework in a little while, and then I'll hand _____ _____.

2. My father is a very smart man. I really look _____ _____ _____.

3. I haven't talked to Aunt Shirley lately. I hope I hear _____ _____ soon.

4. My English teacher didn't like my composition. I have to do _____ _____.

5. I don't know the definition of this word. I need to look _____ _____.

6. I can't find any flour. I think we ran _____ _____ _____.

7. I can't find my wallet. Could you help me look _____ _____?

8. Don't leave your clothes on the bed. You really should hang _____ _____.

9. Don't worry about your mistakes. You can always cross _____ _____.

10. I can never remember Alan's address. I should write _____ _____.

11. I've had the flu for the past several days. My doctor says I'll get _____ _____ soon.

B. Complete the sentences.

so	too	neither	either

Ex. Maria did well on her science test, and ___so did___ her sister.

1. I'm wearing new shoes today, and _____ my brother.

2. I won't be able to come to the meeting tomorrow, and _____ Barbara.

3. I was bored during Professor Gray's lecture, and my friends _____.

4. Janet can't skate, and her brother _____.

5. I've been taking guitar lessons for years, and _____ my sisters.

6. David worked overtime yesterday, and his wife _____.

7. Louise has never been to Europe, and _____ her husband.

8. I want to complain to the landlord, and _____ my neighbors.

9. I'm not very athletic, and _____ my wife.

C. Listen and complete the sentences.

Ex. but her husband ___doesn't___ .

1. but my sister _____ .

2. but my parents _____ .

3. but my brother _____ .

4. but my wife _____ .

5. but I _____ .

Listening Scripts

Listen to each question and then complete the answer.

1. Does Jim like to play soccer?
2. Is Alice working today?
3. Are those students staying after school today?
4. Do Mr. and Mrs. Jackson work hard?
5. Does your wife still write poetry?
6. Is it raining?
7. Is he busy?
8. Do you have to leave?
9. Does your sister play the violin?
10. Is your brother studying in the library?
11. Are you wearing a necklace today?
12. Do you and your husband go camping very often?
13. Is your niece doing her homework?
14. Are they still chatting online?
15. Do you and your friends play Scrabble very often?

Page 13 Exercise B

Listen and circle the correct answer.

1. They work.
2. They worked.
3. We study English.
4. I waited for the bus.
5. We visit our friends.
6. She met important people.
7. He taught Chinese.
8. She delivers the mail.
9. I wrote letters to my friends.
10. I ride my bicycle to work.
11. He sleeps very well.
12. I had a terrible headache.

Page 26 Exercise C

Listen and choose the time of the action.

1. My daughter is going to sing Broadway show tunes in her high school show.
2. Janet bought a new dress for her friend's party.
3. Are you going to go out with George?
4. I went shopping at the new mall.
5. How did you poke yourself in the eye?
6. Who's going to prepare dinner?
7. Did the baby sleep well?
8. I'm really looking forward to Saturday night.
9. Is your son going to play games on his computer?
10. We're going to complain to the landlord about the heat in our apartment.
11. We bought a dozen donuts.
12. I'm going to take astronomy.

Page 33 Exercise L

Listen to each story. Then answer the questions.

What Are Mr. and Mrs. Miller Looking Forward to?

Mr. and Mrs. Miller moved into their new house in Los Angeles last week. They're happy because the house has a large, bright living room and a big, beautiful yard. They're looking forward to life in their new home. Every weekend they'll be able to relax in their living room and enjoy the beautiful California weather in their big, beautiful yard. But this weekend Mr. and Mrs. Miller won't be relaxing. They're going to be very busy. First, they're going to repaint the living room. Then, they're going to assemble their new

computer and VCR. And finally, they're going to plant some flowers in their yard. They'll finally be able to relax NEXT weekend.

What's Jonathan Looking Forward to?

I'm so excited! I'm sitting at my computer in my office, but I'm not thinking about my work today. I'm thinking about next weekend because next Saturday is the day I'll be getting married. After the wedding, my wife and I will be going to Hawaii for a week. I can't wait! For one week, we won't be working, we won't be cooking, we won't be cleaning, and we won't be paying bills. We'll be swimming in the ocean, relaxing on the beach, and eating in fantastic restaurants.

What's Mrs. Grant Looking Forward to?

Mrs. Grant is going to retire this year, and she's really looking forward to her new life. She won't be getting up early every morning and taking the bus to work. She'll be able to sleep late every day of the week. She'll read books, she'll work in her garden, and she'll go to museums with her friends. And she's very happy that she'll be able to spend more time with her grandchildren. She'll take them to the park to feed the birds, she'll take them to the zoo to see the animals, and she'll baby-sit when her son and daughter-in-law go out on Saturday nights.

Page 35 Exercise E

Listen to each question and then complete the answer.

Ex. Does your brother like to swim?
1. Are you going to buy donuts tomorrow?
2. Will Jennifer and John see each other again soon?
3. Doctor, did I sprain my ankle?
4. Does Tommy have a black eye?
5. Is your daughter practicing the violin?
6. Do you and your husband go to the movies very often?
7. Does Diane go out with her boyfriend every Saturday evening?
8. Will you and your wife be visiting us tonight?

Page 36 Exercise B

Listen and choose the word you hear.

1. I've ridden them for many years.
2. Yes. I've taken French.
3. I'm giving injections.
4. I've driven one for many years.
5. Yes. I've written it.
6. I'm drawing it right now.
7. I've spoken it for many years.
8. Yes. I've drawn that.

Page 37 Exercise D

Is Speaker B answering Yes or No? Listen to each conversation and circle the correct answer.

1. A. Do you know how to drive a bus?
   B. I've driven a bus for many years.
2. A. I usually take the train to work. Do you also take the train?
   B. Actually, I've never taken the train to work.
3. A. Are you a good swimmer?
   B. To tell the truth, I've never swum very well.
4. A. Did you get up early this morning?
   B. I've gotten up early every morning this week.

5. A. I'm going to give my dog a bath today. Do you have any advice?
   B. Sorry. I don't. I've never given my dog a bath.
6. A. Do you like to eat sushi?
   B. Of course! I've eaten sushi for many years.
7. A. I just got a big raise! Did you also get one?
   B. Actually, I've never gotten a raise.
8. A. I did very well on the math exam. How about you?
   B. I've never done well on a math exam.

Page 47 Exercise O

What things have these people done? What haven't they done? Listen and check Yes *or* No.

1. A. Carla, have you done your homework yet?
   B. Yes, I have. I did my homework this morning.
   A. And have you practiced the violin?
   B. No, I haven't practiced yet. I promise I'll practice this afternoon.
2. A. Kevin?
   B. Yes, Mrs. Blackwell?
   A. Have you written your report yet?
   B. No, I haven't. I'll write it immediately.
   A. And have you sent a fax to the Crane Company?
   B. No, I haven't. I promise I'll send them a fax after I write the report.
3. A. Have you fed the dog yet?
   B. Yes, I have. I fed him a few minutes ago.
   A. Good. Well, I guess we can leave for work now.
   B. But we haven't eaten breakfast yet!
4. A. I'm leaving now, Mr. Green.
   B. Have you fixed the pipes in the basement, Charlie?
   A. Yes, I have.
   B. And have you repaired the washing machine?
   A. Yes, I have. It's working again.
   B. That's great! Thank you, Charlie.
   A. I'll send you a bill, Mr. Green.
5. A. You know, we haven't done the laundry all week.
   B. I know. We should do it today.
   A. We also haven't vacuumed the rugs!
   B. We haven't?
   A. No, we haven't.
   B. Oh. I guess we should vacuum them today.
6. A. Are we ready for the party?
   B. I think so. We've gotten all the food at the supermarket, and we've cleaned the house from top to bottom!
   A. Well, I guess we're ready for the party!
7. A. Have you spoken to the landlord about our broken light?
   B. Yes, I have. I spoke to him this morning.
   A. What did he say?
   B. He said we should call an electrician.
   A. Okay. Let's call Ajax Electric.
   B. Don't worry. I've already called them, and they're coming this afternoon.
8. A. Have you hooked up the new VCR yet?
   B. I can't do it. It's really difficult.
   A. Have you read the instructions?
   B. Yes, I have. I've read them ten times, and I still can't understand them!

Page 56 Exercise E

Listen and choose the correct answer.

1. Bob has been engaged since he got out of the army.
2. My sister Carol has been a professional musician since she finished music school.
3. Michael has been home since he fell and hurt himself last week.
4. My wife has gotten up early every morning since she started her new job.
5. Richard has eaten breakfast in the school cafeteria every morning since he started college.
6. Nancy and Tom have known each other for five and a half years.
7. My friend Charlie and I have played soccer every weekend since we were eight years old.
8. Patty has had short hair since she was a teenager.
9. Ron has owned his own business since he moved to Chicago nine years ago.
10. I've been interested in astronomy for the past eleven years.
11. I use my personal computer all the time. I've had it since I was in high school.
12. Alan has had problems with his house since he bought it fifteen years ago.

Page 61 Exercise L

Listen and choose the correct answer.

1. A. Have you always been a salesperson?
   B. No. I've been a salesperson for the past four years. Before that, I was a cashier.
2. A. How long has your daughter been in medical school?
   B. She's been in medical school for the past two years.
3. A. Have your parents always lived in a house?
   B. No. They've lived in a house for the past ten years. Before that, they lived in an apartment.
4. A. How long have you wanted to be an actor?
   B. I've wanted to be an actor since I was in college. Before that, I wanted to be a musician.
5. A. Do you and your husband still exercise at your health club every day?
   B. No. We haven't done that for a year.
6. A. Has James been a bachelor all his life?
   B. No, he hasn't. He was married for ten years.
7. A. Has your sister Jane always wanted to be a writer?
   B. Yes, she has. She's wanted to be a writer all her life.
8. A. Have you ever broken your ankle?
   B. No. I've sprained it a few times, but I've never broken it.
9. A. Have you always liked classical music?
   B. No. I've liked classical music for the past few years. Before that, I liked rock music.
10. A. Has Billy had a sore throat for a long time?
    B. He's had a sore throat for the past two days. Before that, he had a fever.
11. A. Jennifer has been the store manager since last fall.
    B. What did she do before that?
    A. She was a salesperson.

12. A. Have you always been interested in modern art?
    B. No. I've been interested in modern art since I moved to Paris a few years ago. Before that, I was only interested in sports.

Page 64 Exercise E

Listen and choose the correct time expressions to complete the sentences.

1. A. How long have you been living there?
   B. I've been living there since . . .

2. A. How long has your daughter been practicing the piano?
   B. She's been practicing for . . .

3. A. How long have I been running?
   B. You've been running since . . .

4. A. How long have you been feeling bad?
   B. I've been feeling bad for . . .

5. A. How long have they been waiting?
   B. They've been waiting for . . .

6. A. How long has your son been studying?
   B. He's been studying since . . .

7. A. How long have your sister and her boyfriend been dating?
   B. They've been dating since . . .

8. A. Dad, how long have we been driving?
   B. Hmm. I think we've been driving for . . .

9. A. How long has your little girl been crying?
   B. She's been crying for . . .

Page 67 Exercise H

Listen and choose what the people are talking about.

1. She's been directing it for an hour.
2. We've been rearranging it all morning.
3. I've been paying them on time.
4. He's been playing them for years.
5. Have you been bathing them for a long time?
6. They've been rebuilding it for a year.
7. She's been writing it for a week.
8. He's been translating them for many years.
9. I've been reading it all afternoon.
10. She's been knitting them for a few weeks.
11. We've been listening to them all afternoon.
12. I've been recommending it for years.
13. They've been repairing it all day.
14. She's been taking it all morning.
15. I've been solving them all my life.

Page 71 Exercise L

Listen and decide where the conversation is taking place.

1. A. I'm really tired.
   B. No wonder! You've been chopping tomatoes for the past hour.

2. A. Mark! I'm surprised. You've been falling asleep in class all morning, and you've never fallen asleep in class before.
   B. I'm sorry, Mrs. Applebee. It won't happen again.

3. A. I've been washing these shirts for the past half hour, and they still aren't clean.
   B. Here. Try this Presto Soap.

4. A. We've been standing in line for an hour and forty-five minutes.
   B. I know. I hope the movie is good. I've never stood in line for such a long time.

5. A. What seems to be the problem, Mr. Jones?
   B. My back has been hurting me for the past few days.
   A. I'm sorry to hear that.

6. A. You know, we've been reading here for more than two hours.
   B. You're right. I think it's time to go now.

7. A. Do you want to leave?
   B. I think so. We've seen all the paintings here.

8. A. How long have you been exercising?
   B. For an hour and a half.

9. A. We've been waiting for an hour, and it still isn't here.
   B. I know. I'm going to be late for work.

10. A. I think we've seen them all. Which one do you want to buy?
    B. I like that black one over there.

11. A. We've been watching this movie for the past hour, and it's terrible!
    B. You're right. Let's change the channel.

12. A. I've got a terrible headache.
    B. Why?
    A. Customers have been complaining all morning.
    B. What have they been complaining about?
    A. Some people have been complaining about our terrible products, but most people have been complaining about our high prices.

Page 77 Exercise F

Listen and choose the correct answer.

1. A. How long has Janet been an actress?
   B. She's been an actress since she graduated from acting school.

2. A. Have you watched the news yet?
   B. Yes. I saw the president, and I heard his speech.

3. A. Have you always lived in Denver?
   B. No. We've lived in Denver since 1995. Before that, we lived in New York.

4. A. Has Dad made dinner yet?
   B. Not yet. He still has to make it.

5. A. How long has your ceiling been leaking?
   B. It's been leaking for more than a week.
   A. Have you called the superintendent?
   B. Yes, I have. I've called him several times.

6. A. Billy is having trouble with his homework.
   B. Has he asked anyone to help him?
   A. No, he hasn't.

Page 87 Exercise N

Listen and choose the correct answer.

1. Dr. Gomez really enjoys . . .
2. Whenever possible, my wife and I try to avoid . . .
3. Next summer I'm going to learn . . .
4. Every day Rita practices . . .
5. My parents have decided . . .
6. I've considered . . .
7. Are you thinking about . . .
8. I'm going to quit . . .
9. Why do you keep on . . .
10. My doctor says I should stop . . .
11. David can't stand . . .
12. Are you going to continue to . . .

13. James doesn't want to start . . .
14. Next semester Kathy is going to begin . . .
15. You know, you can't keep on . . .

Page 97 Exercise J

Listen and choose the correct answer.

1. Steve lost his voice.
2. Is Beverly one of your relatives?
3. We just canceled our trip to South America.
4. Ricky has been failing all of his tests this year.
5. Francine dislocated her shoulder.
6. What did you and your students discuss in class?
7. My girlfriend and I rode on the roller coaster yesterday.
8. Grandma can't chew this piece of steak very well.
9. Jimmy loves my homemade food.
10. Did you see the motorcycles go by?
11. Do you think Mr. Montero will take a day off soon?
12. Amy wanted to ask her boss for a raise, but she got cold feet.
13. Have you heard that Margaret sprained her wrist?
14. I have to make an important decision.
15. I envy you.
16. I feel terrible. Debbie and Dan broke up last week.
17. My ankle hurts a lot.
18. I was heartbroken when I heard what happened.
19. Michael was furious with his neighbors.
20. We went to a recital last night.
21. Tom, don't forget to shine your shoes!
22. My friend Carla is extremely athletic.
23. My husband and I have been writing invitations all afternoon.
24. Charles rented a beautiful tuxedo for his niece's wedding.

Page 99 Exercise D

Listen and choose the correct answer.

Ex. My grandfather likes to . . .
1. Susan says she's going to stop . . .
2. My wife and I are thinking about . . .
3. David is considering . . .
4. I can't stand to . . .
5. You should definitely keep on . . .

Page 105 Exercise G

Listen and choose the correct answer.

1. A. I looked in the refrigerator, and I can't find the orange juice.
   B. That's because we . . .

2. A. I'm frustrated! My computer isn't working today.
   B. I think you forgot to . . .

3. A. What should I do with the Christmas decorations?
   B. I think it's time to . . .

4. A. Should I take these clothes to the cleaner's?
   B. Yes. You should definitely . . .

5. A. Hmm. What does this word mean?
   B. You should . . .

6. A. I have to return this skateboard to my cousin.
   B. When are you going to . . . ?

7. A. This math problem is very difficult.
   B. Maybe I can . . .

8. A. I'll never remember their new telephone number.
   B. You should . . .

9. A. I just spilled milk on the kitchen floor!
   B. Don't worry. I'll . . .

Page 108 Exercise L

Listen and choose the correct answer.

1. I really look up to my father.
2. My brother picks on me all the time.
3. Did you throw away the last can of paint?
4. I still haven't gotten over the flu.
5. Have you heard from your cousin Sam recently?
6. Why did you turn him down?
7. Did your French teacher call on you today?
8. George picked out a new suit for his wedding.
9. I have to drop my sister off at the airport.
10. Everything in the store is 20 percent off this week.
11. This jacket fits you.
12. Did you try on a lot of shoes?

Page 112 Exercise D

Listen and complete the sentences.

1. I missed the bus this morning.
2. I'm allergic to nuts.
3. I'll be on vacation next week.
4. I've never flown in a helicopter.
5. I can speak Chinese.
6. I like to go sailing.
7. I'm not going to the company picnic this weekend.
8. I saw a very good movie last night.
9. I don't go on many business trips.
10. I've been to London several times.
11. I'm not a vegetarian.
12. I should lose a little weight.
13. I can't stop worrying about my health.
14. I hate to drive downtown.
15. I won't be able to go to Nancy's party this Saturday night.

Page 117 Exercise K

Listen and complete the sentences.

1. I missed the bus today, . . .
2. I'm allergic to cats, . . .
3. I'll be on vacation next week, . . .
4. You've never seen a rainbow, . . .
5. I can speak Italian, . . .
6. I like to go sailing, . . .
7. I've been on television several times, . . .
8. I saw an exciting movie last weekend, . . .
9. I won't be in the office tomorrow, . . .
10. We were late, . . .
11. I'm not a vegetarian, . . .
12. I saw the stop sign, . . .
13. I can't swim very well, . . .
14. They have to work overtime this weekend, . . .
15. I won't be able to go to Sam's party this Friday night, . . .
16. I'm not afraid of flying, . . .
17. I haven't eaten breakfast yet, . . .
18. The other students weren't bored, . . .

Page 121 Exercise C

Listen and complete the sentences.

Ex. Nancy knows how to type, . . .
1. I'm interested in science, . . .
2. I won't be home this evening, . . .
3. I own my own business, . . .
4. I've never hooked up a computer, . . .
5. You just got a raise, . . .

Correlation Key

Student Text Pages	Activity Workbook Pages	Student Text Pages	Activity Workbook Pages
Chapter 1		**Chapter 7**	
2	2–3	82	78–79
3	4–5	84	80–81
4	6–8	86–87	82
7–8	9–11	88–89	83–84
		90–91	85–87
Chapter 2			
12	12–13	**Chapter 8**	
13	14–17	96–97	88–89
14–15	18–19	100	90
18–19	20–23	101	91
		104–105	92–93
Chapter 3		106–107	94–96
22–23	24–26	109	97
25	27		
26	28–29	**Check-Up Test**	**98–99**
27	30		
28–29	31–33	**Chapter 9**	
		116	100
Check-Up Test	**34–35**	117	101–102
		119	103
Chapter 4		122–123	104–105
38	36	124	106–107
39	37	126–127	108
40	38		
41	39	**Chapter 10**	
42–43	40–43	132	109–110
45	44–45	133	111–112
46	46–47	134–135	113
48	48–50	138–139	114–115
50	51	141	116–117
		143	118–119
Chapter 5			
52–53	52–54	**Check-Up Test**	**120–121**
56–57	55–57		
58–59	58–59		
62–63	60–61		
Chapter 6			
70–71	62–65		
72	66–68		
74–75	69–71		
76–77	72–75		
Check-Up Test	**76–77**		